SUPER CUTAWAYS

SPACECRAFT AND AIRCRAFT

Written by Ian Graham

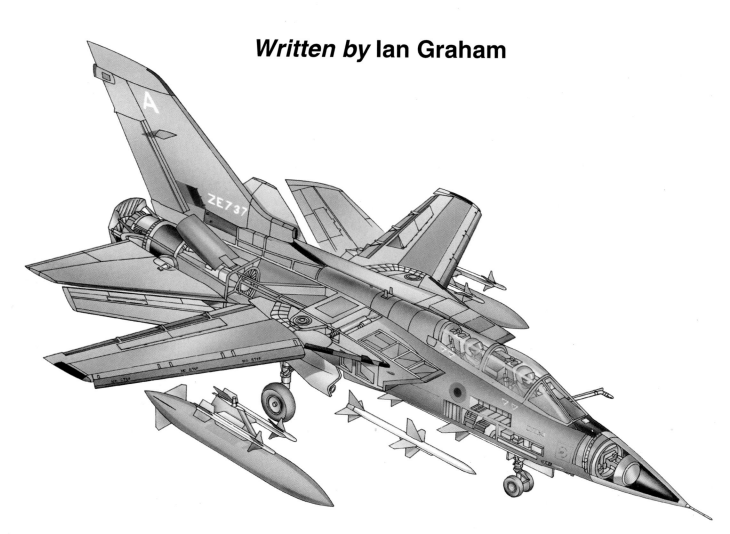

DERRYDALE BOOKS
NEW YORK • AVENEL

Acknowledgments

Illustrated by
Ian Moores
Roger Stewart

Picture Credits
9 TRH Pictures **10** Aviation Picture Library/Austin J Brown
13 Quadrant Picture Library/Tony Hobbs **14** Ian Graham
20 TRH Pictures/US Air Force **22** Genesis Space Photo
Library **24** TRH Pictures/NASA **27** Science Photo
Library/NASA **28** Science Photo Library/NASA **33** Genesis
Space Photo Library/Novosti

This 1995 edition published by Derrydale Books, distributed by
Random House Value Publishing, Inc., 40 Engelhard Avenue,
Avenel, New Jersey 07001

Random House
New York • Toronto • London • Sydney • Auckland

Planned and Produced by
Andromeda Oxford Limited
11-15 The Vineyard
Abingdon
Oxon OX14 3PX

Copyright © Andromeda Oxford Limited 1995

ISBN 0-517-14065-9
Printed in Italy by Graphicom

Contents

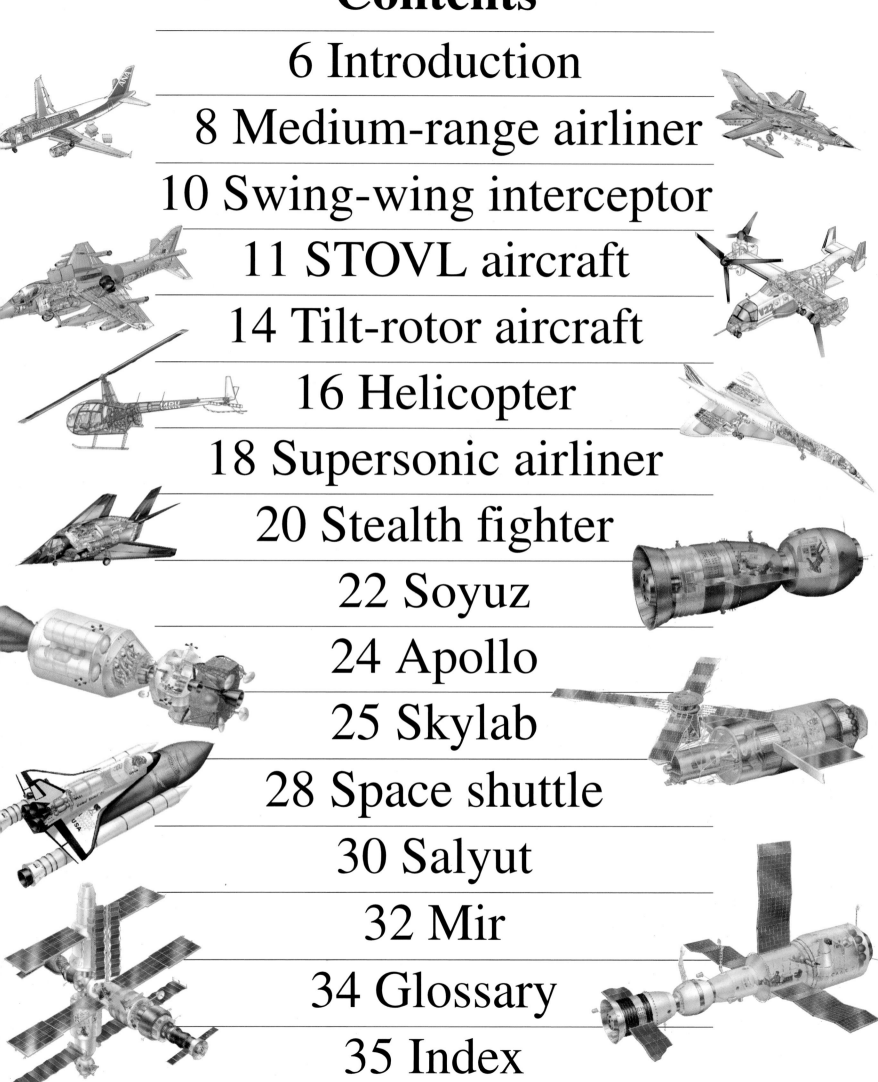

Introduction

AIRCRAFT AND SPACECRAFT are both types of machines that can take off from the land and travel through the sky, but they have many important differences. Aircraft fly within Earth's atmosphere, and use the flow of air rushing over their wings to maintain lift. Some aircraft are used to carry people and cargo from place to place, some are used for fighting and others are used for special tasks such as crop spraying or observation. Spacecraft are machines that fly into space. They are always launched from Earth by rockets. Because there is no air in space, spacecraft do not have wings. Instead, they use the power from their rockets to thrust them through space. Spacecraft are used to discover more about the stars and planets, to find out what effect space travel has on humans, and to carry out other experiments.

In this book you will find out about many of the most important types of aircraft and spacecraft. Each craft is illustrated to show what it is like inside and also how it works.

Introductory Text

The introductory text tells the story of each aircraft or spacecraft. For example, it explains when it was built, how it works and what its special features are.

Working Diagrams

Working diagrams focus on one particular feature of the central image – for example, Concorde's 'droop-snoot'. The diagrams give clear visual explanations of what these important features do and how they work.

Supersonic airliner

A SUPERSONIC AIRCRAFT fl[...] speed of sound. The jet-powere[...] 1950s flew as fast as 621mph ([...] than their propeller-driven predecessors. [...] aircraft were designed which could fly f[...] sound. The world's first supersonic airlin[...] joint production by the French and Britis[...] The slim, paper dart wing shape and fou[...] enable Concorde to fly high in the atmo[...] speed of sound. Its top speed of 1450mp[...] faster than many jet fighters. When flyi[...] Atlantic, it crosses the sky faster than th[...] possible for travellers to arrive on the o[...] earlier than the time they left! You can l[...] and arrive in New York at 9a.m. on the [...] times, of course). The journey only take[...] half the time taken by a long-range airl[...] 747. Concorde flies at a height of 59,0[...] twice as high as a subsonic airliner. Al[...] 1969 and entered service in 1976, Con[...] supersonic airliner in service.

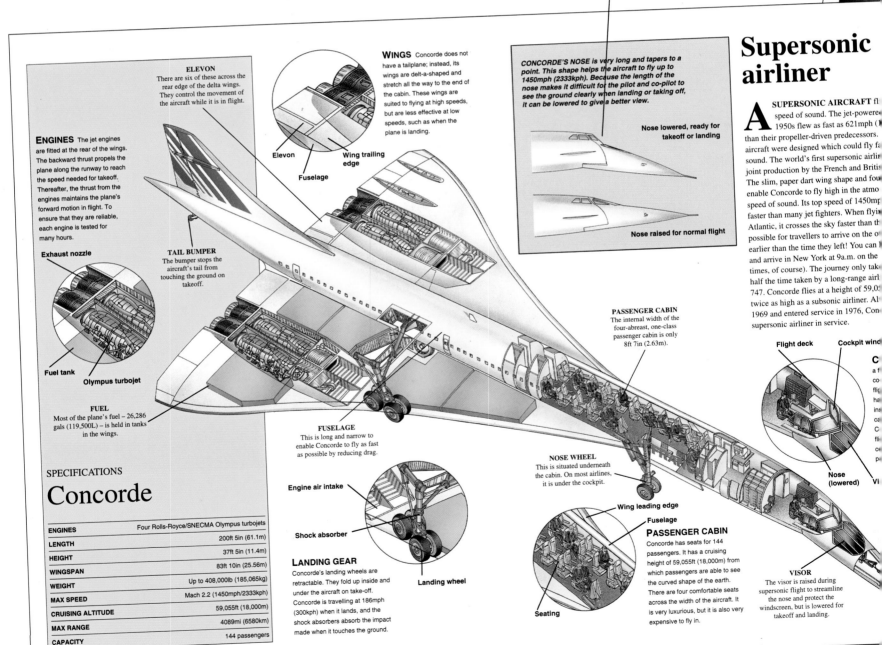

ELEVON
There are six of these across the rear edge of the delta wings. They control the movement of the aircraft while it is in flight.

WINGS Concorde does not have a tailplane; instead, its wings are delt-a-shaped and stretch all the way to the end of the cabin. These wings are suited to flying at high speeds, but are less effective at low speeds, such as when the plane is landing.

Elevon

Wing trailing edge

Fuselage

CONCORDE'S NOSE is very long and tapers to a point. This shape helps the aircraft to fly up to 1450mph (2333kph). Because the length of the nose makes it difficult for the pilot and co-pilot to see the ground clearly when landing or taking off, it can be lowered to give a better view.

Nose lowered, ready for takeoff or landing

Nose raised for normal flight

ENGINES The jet engines are fitted at the rear of the wings. The backward thrust propels the plane along the runway to reach the speed needed for takeoff. Thereafter, the thrust from the engines maintains the plane's forward motion in flight. To ensure that they are reliable, each engine is tested for many hours.

Exhaust nozzle

TAIL BUMPER
The bumper stops the aircraft's tail from touching the ground on takeoff.

Fuel tank

Olympus turbojet

FUEL
Most of the plane's fuel – 26,286 gals (119,500L) – is held in tanks in the wings.

PASSENGER CABIN
The internal width of the four-abreast, one-class passenger cabin is only 8ft 7in (2.63m).

Flight deck

Cockpit wind[...]

C[...]
a fl[...]
co[...]
fli[...]
ha[...]
ins[...]
ca[...]
C[...]
fli[...]
c[...]
p[...]

Nose (lowered)

Vi[...]

FUSELAGE
This is long and narrow to enable Concorde to fly as fast as possible by reducing drag.

Engine air intake

Shock absorber

NOSE WHEEL
This is situated underneath the cabin. On most airlines, it is under the cockpit.

Wing leading edge

Fuselage

PASSENGER CABIN
Concorde has seats for 144 passengers. It has a cruising height of 59,055ft (18,000m) from which passengers are able to see the curved shape of the earth. There are four comfortable seats across the width of the aircraft. It is very luxurious, but it is also very expensive to fly in.

Seating

LANDING GEAR
Concorde's landing wheels are retractable. They fold up inside and under the aircraft on take-off. Concorde is travelling at 186mph (300kph) when it lands, and the shock absorbers absorb the impact made when it touches the ground.

Landing wheel

VISOR
The visor is raised during supersonic flight to streamline the nose and protect the windscreen, but is lowered for takeoff and landing.

SPECIFICATIONS

Concorde

ENGINES	Four Rolls-Royce/SNECMA Olympus turbojets
LENGTH	200ft 5in (61.1m)
HEIGHT	37ft 5in (11.4m)
WINGSPAN	83ft 10in (25.56m)
WEIGHT	Up to 408,000lb (185,065kg)
MAX SPEED	Mach 2.2 (1450mph/2333kph)
CRUISING ALTITUDE	59,055ft (18,000m)
MAX RANGE	4089mi (6580km)
CAPACITY	144 passengers

18

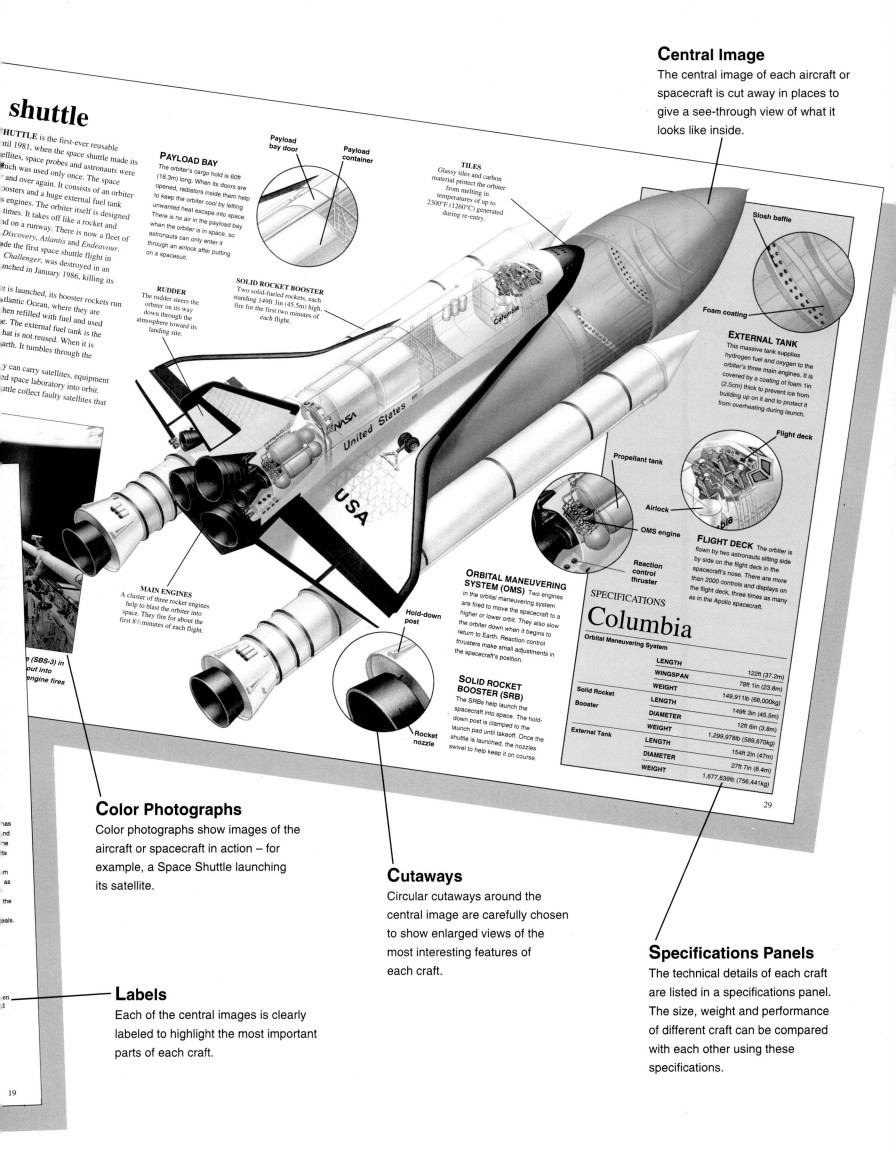

shuttle

HUTTLE is the first-ever reusable
ntil 1981, when the space shuttle made its
ellites, space probes and astronauts were
hich was used only once. The space
r and over again. It consists of an orbiter
oosters and a huge external fuel tank
s engines. The orbiter itself is designed
times. It takes off like an airplane and
d on a runway. There is now a fleet of
Discovery, Atlantis and *Endeavour.*
de the first space shuttle flight in
Challenger, was destroyed in an
nched in January 1986, killing its

e is launched, its booster rockets run
tlantic Ocean, where they are
hen refilled with fuel and used
e. The external fuel tank is the
hat is not reused. When it is
arth. It tumbles through the

y can carry satellites, equipment
ed space laboratory into orbit.
ttle collect faulty satellites that

e (SBS-3) in
out into
engine fires

has
nd
he
ts

m

as

the

als.

en
d

Central Image
The central image of each aircraft or
spacecraft is cut away in places to
give a see-through view of what it
looks like inside.

PAYLOAD BAY
The orbiter's cargo hold is 60ft
(18.3m) long. When its doors are
opened, radiators inside them help
to keep the orbiter cool by letting
unwanted heat escape into space.
There is no air in the payload bay
when the orbiter is in space, so
astronauts can only enter it
through an airlock after putting
on a spacesuit.

Payload bay door

Payload container

TILES
Glassy tiles and carbon
material protect the orbiter
from melting in
temperatures of up to
2300°F (1260°C) generated
during re-entry.

Slosh baffle

Foam coating

EXTERNAL TANK
This massive tank supplies
hydrogen fuel and oxygen to the
orbiter's three main engines. It is
covered by a coating of foam 1in
(2.5cm) thick to prevent ice from
building up on it and to protect it
from overheating during launch.

RUDDER
The rudder steers the
orbiter on its way
down through the
atmosphere toward its
landing site.

SOLID ROCKET BOOSTER
Two solid-fueled rockets, each
standing 149ft 3in (45.5m) high,
fire for the first two minutes of
each flight.

Flight deck

Propellant tank

Airlock

OMS engine

Reaction control thruster

FLIGHT DECK The orbiter is
flown by two astronauts sitting side
by side on the flight deck in the
spacecraft's nose. There are more
than 2000 controls and displays on
the flight deck, three times as many
as in the Apollo spacecraft.

MAIN ENGINES
A cluster of three rocket engines
help to blast the orbiter into
space. They fire for about the
first 8½ minutes of each flight.

Hold-down post

**ORBITAL MANEUVERING
SYSTEM (OMS)** Two engines
in the orbital maneuvering system
are fired to move the spacecraft to a
higher or lower orbit. They also slow
the orbiter down when it begins to
return to Earth. Reaction control
thrusters make small adjustments in
the spacecraft's position.

**SOLID ROCKET
BOOSTER (SRB)**
The SRBs help launch the
spacecraft into space. The hold-
down post is clamped to the
launch pad until takeoff. Once the
shuttle is launched, the nozzles
swivel to help keep it on course.

Rocket nozzle

SPECIFICATIONS

Columbia

Orbital Maneuvering System

	LENGTH	122ft (37.2m)
	WINGSPAN	78ft 1in (23.8m)
Solid Rocket Booster	WEIGHT	149,911lb (68,000kg)
	LENGTH	149ft 3in (45.5m)
	DIAMETER	12ft 6in (3.8m)
External Tank	WEIGHT	1,299,978lb (589,670kg)
	LENGTH	154ft 2in (47m)
	DIAMETER	27ft 7in (8.4m)
	WEIGHT	1,677,639lb (756,441kg)

Color Photographs
Color photographs show images of the
aircraft or spacecraft in action – for
example, a Space Shuttle launching
its satellite.

Cutaways
Circular cutaways around the
central image are carefully chosen
to show enlarged views of the
most interesting features of
each craft.

Specifications Panels
The technical details of each craft
are listed in a specifications panel.
The size, weight and performance
of different craft can be compared
with each other using these
specifications.

Labels
Each of the central images is clearly
labeled to highlight the most important
parts of each craft.

Medium-range airliner

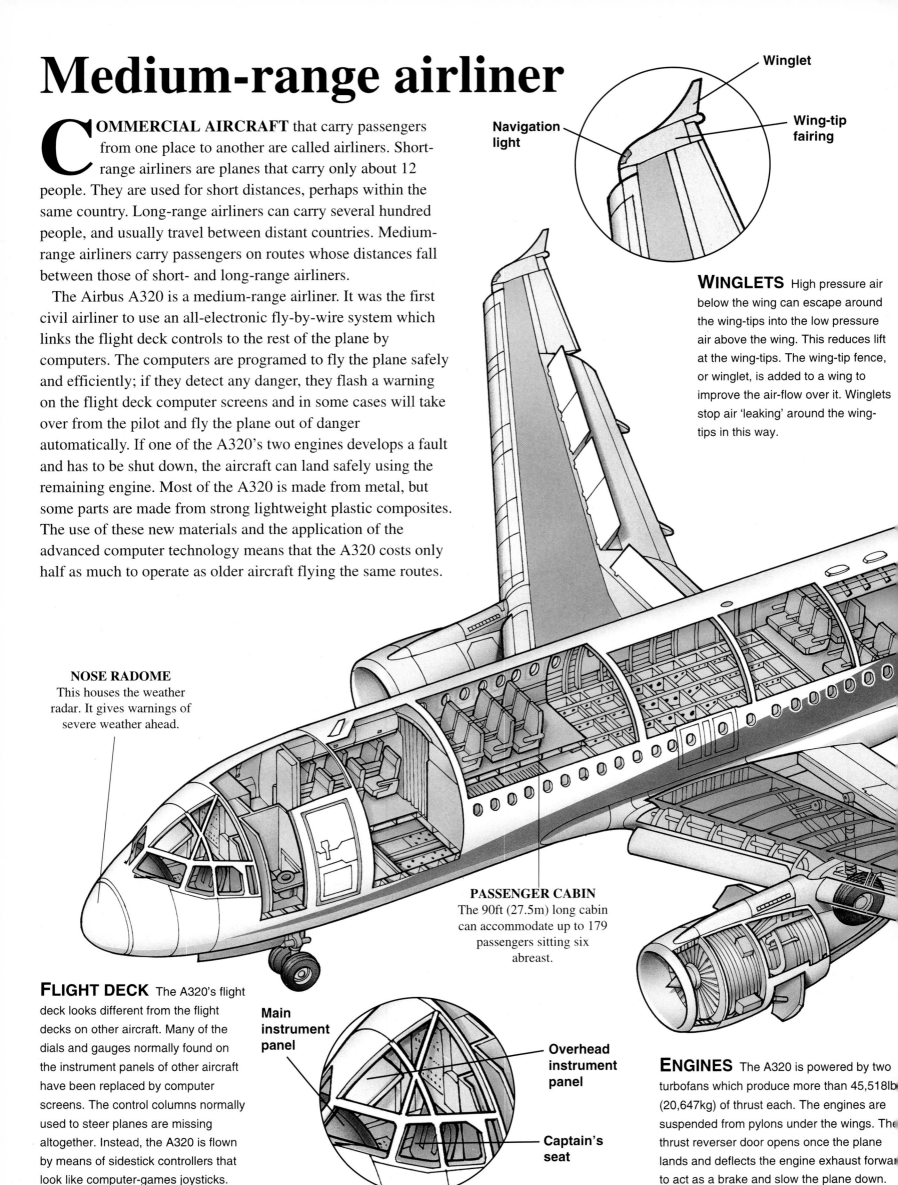

COMMERCIAL AIRCRAFT that carry passengers from one place to another are called airliners. Short-range airliners are planes that carry only about 12 people. They are used for short distances, perhaps within the same country. Long-range airliners can carry several hundred people, and usually travel between distant countries. Medium-range airliners carry passengers on routes whose distances fall between those of short- and long-range airliners.

The Airbus A320 is a medium-range airliner. It was the first civil airliner to use an all-electronic fly-by-wire system which links the flight deck controls to the rest of the plane by computers. The computers are programed to fly the plane safely and efficiently; if they detect any danger, they flash a warning on the flight deck computer screens and in some cases will take over from the pilot and fly the plane out of danger automatically. If one of the A320's two engines develops a fault and has to be shut down, the aircraft can land safely using the remaining engine. Most of the A320 is made from metal, but some parts are made from strong lightweight plastic composites. The use of these new materials and the application of the advanced computer technology means that the A320 costs only half as much to operate as older aircraft flying the same routes.

Navigation light

Winglet

Wing-tip fairing

WINGLETS High pressure air below the wing can escape around the wing-tips into the low pressure air above the wing. This reduces lift at the wing-tips. The wing-tip fence, or winglet, is added to a wing to improve the air-flow over it. Winglets stop air 'leaking' around the wing-tips in this way.

NOSE RADOME
This houses the weather radar. It gives warnings of severe weather ahead.

PASSENGER CABIN
The 90ft (27.5m) long cabin can accommodate up to 179 passengers sitting six abreast.

FLIGHT DECK The A320's flight deck looks different from the flight decks on other aircraft. Many of the dials and gauges normally found on the instrument panels of other aircraft have been replaced by computer screens. The control columns normally used to steer planes are missing altogether. Instead, the A320 is flown by means of sidestick controllers that look like computer-games joysticks.

Main instrument panel

Overhead instrument panel

Captain's seat

ENGINES The A320 is powered by two turbofans which produce more than 45,518lb (20,647kg) of thrust each. The engines are suspended from pylons under the wings. The thrust reverser door opens once the plane lands and deflects the engine exhaust forwar to act as a brake and slow the plane down.

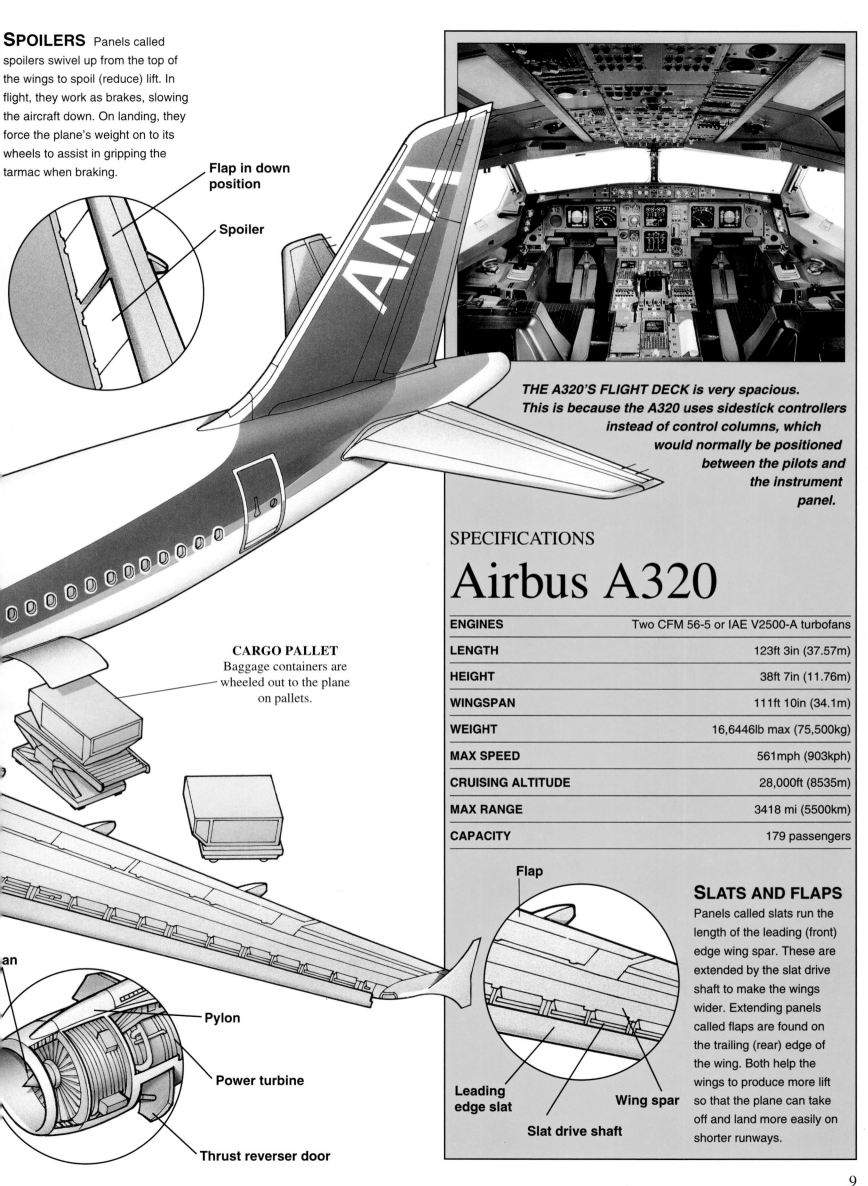

SPOILERS Panels called spoilers swivel up from the top of the wings to spoil (reduce) lift. In flight, they work as brakes, slowing the aircraft down. On landing, they force the plane's weight on to its wheels to assist in gripping the tarmac when braking.

Flap in down position

Spoiler

THE A320'S FLIGHT DECK is very spacious. This is because the A320 uses sidestick controllers instead of control columns, which would normally be positioned between the pilots and the instrument panel.

SPECIFICATIONS

Airbus A320

ENGINES	Two CFM 56-5 or IAE V2500-A turbofans
LENGTH	123ft 3in (37.57m)
HEIGHT	38ft 7in (11.76m)
WINGSPAN	111ft 10in (34.1m)
WEIGHT	16,6446lb max (75,500kg)
MAX SPEED	561mph (903kph)
CRUISING ALTITUDE	28,000ft (8535m)
MAX RANGE	3418 mi (5500km)
CAPACITY	179 passengers

CARGO PALLET
Baggage containers are wheeled out to the plane on pallets.

an

Pylon

Power turbine

Thrust reverser door

Flap

SLATS AND FLAPS
Panels called slats run the length of the leading (front) edge wing spar. These are extended by the slat drive shaft to make the wings wider. Extending panels called flaps are found on the trailing (rear) edge of the wing. Both help the wings to produce more lift so that the plane can take off and land more easily on shorter runways.

Leading edge slat

Slat drive shaft

Wing spar

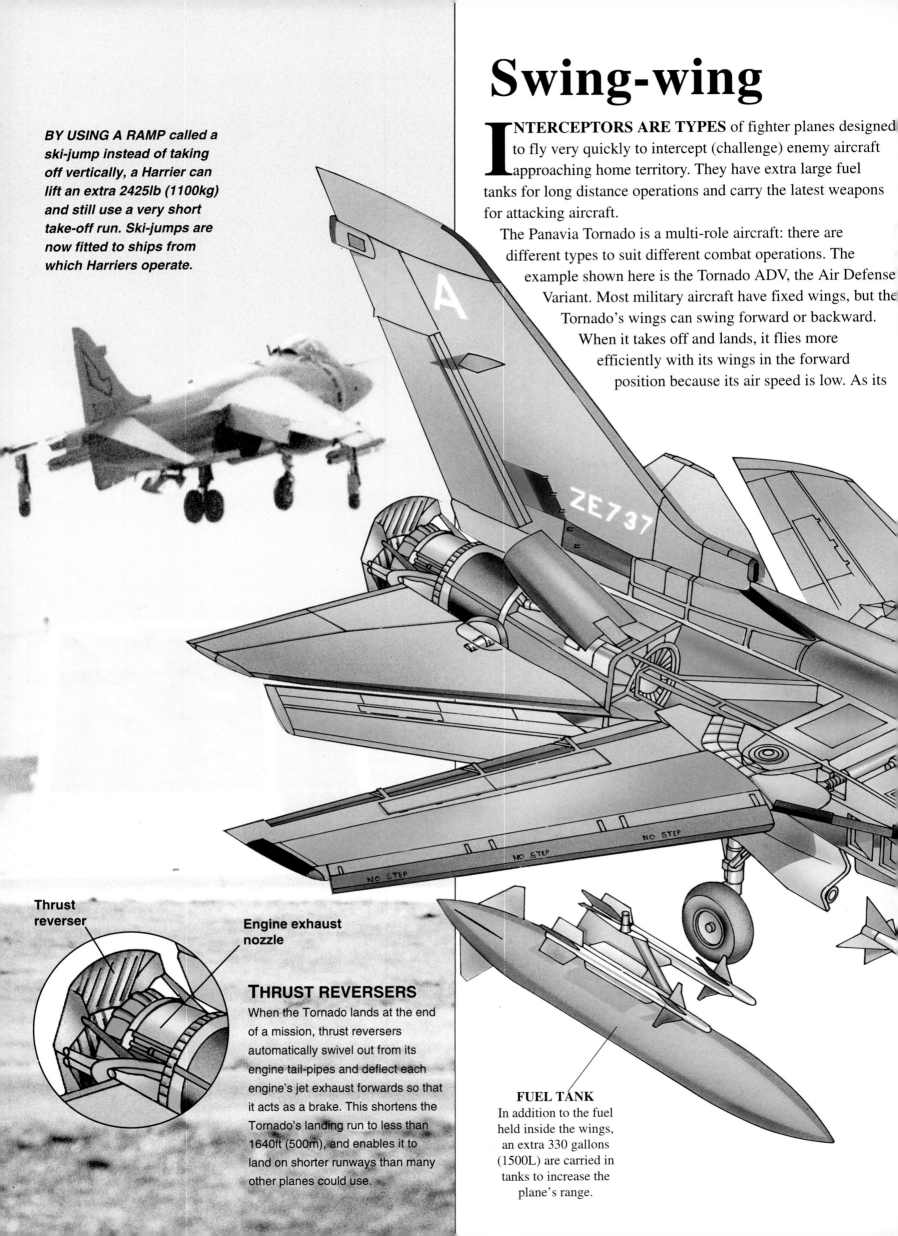

BY USING A RAMP called a ski-jump instead of taking off vertically, a Harrier can lift an extra 2425lb (1100kg) and still use a very short take-off run. Ski-jumps are now fitted to ships from which Harriers operate.

Swing-wing

INTERCEPTORS ARE TYPES of fighter planes designed to fly very quickly to intercept (challenge) enemy aircraft approaching home territory. They have extra large fuel tanks for long distance operations and carry the latest weapons for attacking aircraft.

The Panavia Tornado is a multi-role aircraft: there are different types to suit different combat operations. The example shown here is the Tornado ADV, the Air Defense Variant. Most military aircraft have fixed wings, but the Tornado's wings can swing forward or backward. When it takes off and lands, it flies more efficiently with its wings in the forward position because its air speed is low. As its

Thrust reverser

Engine exhaust nozzle

THRUST REVERSERS

When the Tornado lands at the end of a mission, thrust reversers automatically swivel out from its engine tail-pipes and deflect each engine's jet exhaust forwards so that it acts as a brake. This shortens the Tornado's landing run to less than 1640ft (500m), and enables it to land on shorter runways than many other planes could use.

FUEL TANK
In addition to the fuel held inside the wings, an extra 330 gallons (1500L) are carried in tanks to increase the plane's range.

A TORNADO'S TWO-MAN CREW lower themselves into their ejection seats and strap themselves in. The pilot sits in the front seat and the weapons system operator sits in the rear seat. Ground crew help them into their seats.

SPECIFICATIONS

Panavia Tornado

ENGINES	Two Turbo-Union RB-199 turbofans
LENGTH	61ft 3in (18.68m)
HEIGHT	19ft 6in (5.95m)
WINGSPAN (unswept)	45ft 7in (13.91m)
WEIGHT	Up to 62,830lb (28,500kg)
MAX SPEED	Mach 2.2 (1450mph/2333kph)
SERVICE CEILING	70,000ft (21,335m)
MAX RANGE	1118mi (1800km)
WEAPONS	27mm cannon, Skyflash and Sidewinder missiles

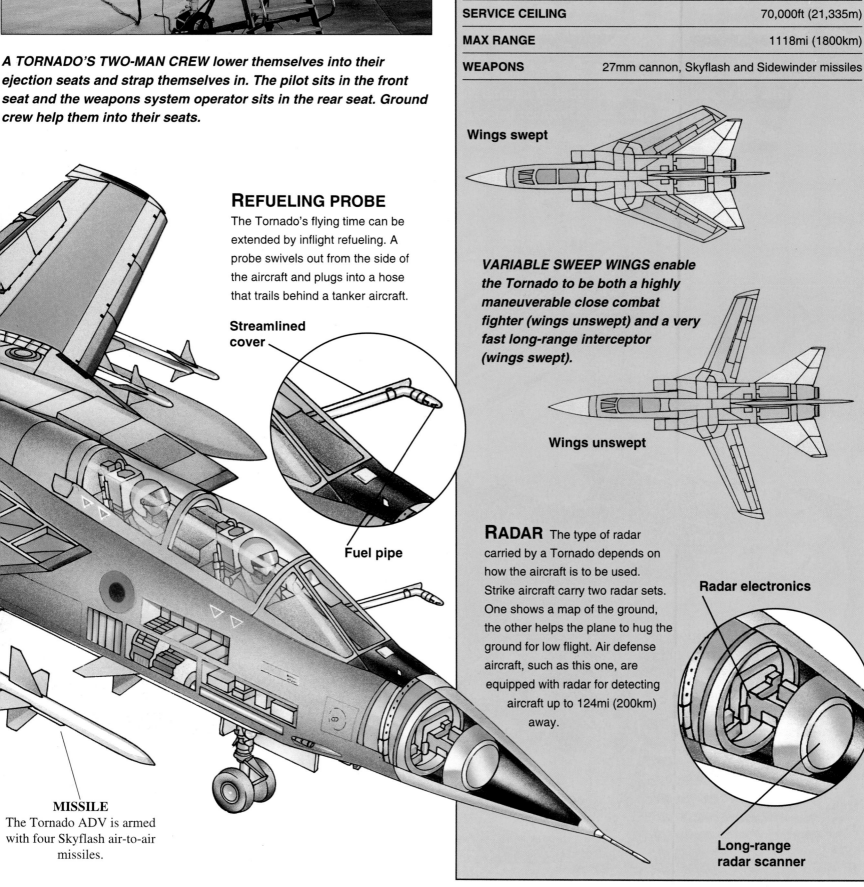

Wings swept

VARIABLE SWEEP WINGS enable the Tornado to be both a highly maneuverable close combat fighter (wings unswept) and a very fast long-range interceptor (wings swept).

Wings unswept

REFUELING PROBE

The Tornado's flying time can be extended by inflight refueling. A probe swivels out from the side of the aircraft and plugs into a hose that trails behind a tanker aircraft.

Streamlined cover

Fuel pipe

RADAR The type of radar carried by a Tornado depends on how the aircraft is to be used. Strike aircraft carry two radar sets. One shows a map of the ground, the other helps the plane to hug the ground for low flight. Air defense aircraft, such as this one, are equipped with radar for detecting aircraft up to 124mi (200km) away.

Radar electronics

MISSILE
The Tornado ADV is armed with four Skyflash air-to-air missiles.

Long-range radar scanner

Tilt-rotor aircraft

HELICOPTERS CAN TAKE OFF and land vertically, but are unable to fly as fast as fixed-wing airplanes. Fixed-wing aircraft are able to fly as fast as their power will allow, but need long runways in order to attain take-off speed and cannot hover. An aircraft which can take off and land vertically and also fly as fast as a fixed-wing airplane combines the most advantageous features of both types of aircraft.

The Tilt-rotor is such an aircraft. It is part helicopter and part airplane. It has wings, like a fixed-wing aircraft, as well as giant rotors like those of a helicopter. These are called proprotors because they are a blend of both propellers and rotors. Once the proprotors have lifted the aircraft off the ground, the engines slowly swivel until the proprotors face forward to work like propellers. They pull the aircraft forward and its wings take over the job of producing lift like a fixed-wing airplane.

Tilt-rotors can be used for transporting troops and equipment and hunting for submarines. They can also be used for search and rescue work. A civilian version will be available to carry passengers.

PROPROTOR Proprotors are much bigger than propellers because they have to work like helicopter rotors and support the 59,535lb (27,443kg) weight of the aircraft during vertical takeoff and landing. The blades are made from a very strong material called graphite-fiberglass.

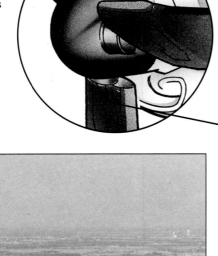

Proprotor hub

Proprotor blade

HOVER MODE
Each engine is attached to the end of the wing by a swiveling joint. When the pilot rotates the engines to vertical, as shown here, the aircraft can hover.

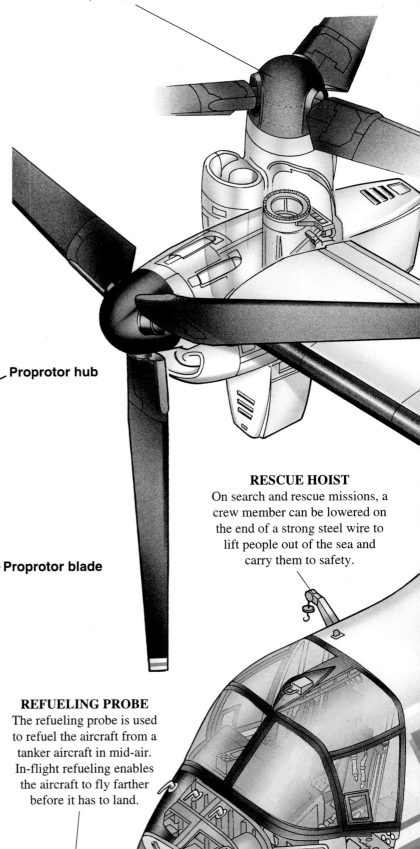

RESCUE HOIST
On search and rescue missions, a crew member can be lowered on the end of a strong steel wire to lift people out of the sea and carry them to safety.

REFUELING PROBE
The refueling probe is used to refuel the aircraft from a tanker aircraft in mid-air. In-flight refueling enables the aircraft to fly farther before it has to land.

THE TILT-ROTOR AIRCRAFT at the top of the picture has twisted its proprotors forward. Its wings are producing lift, and the engines are pulling the aircraft forward. The lower aircraft has rotated its engines upward so that its proprotors lift it higher into the sky.

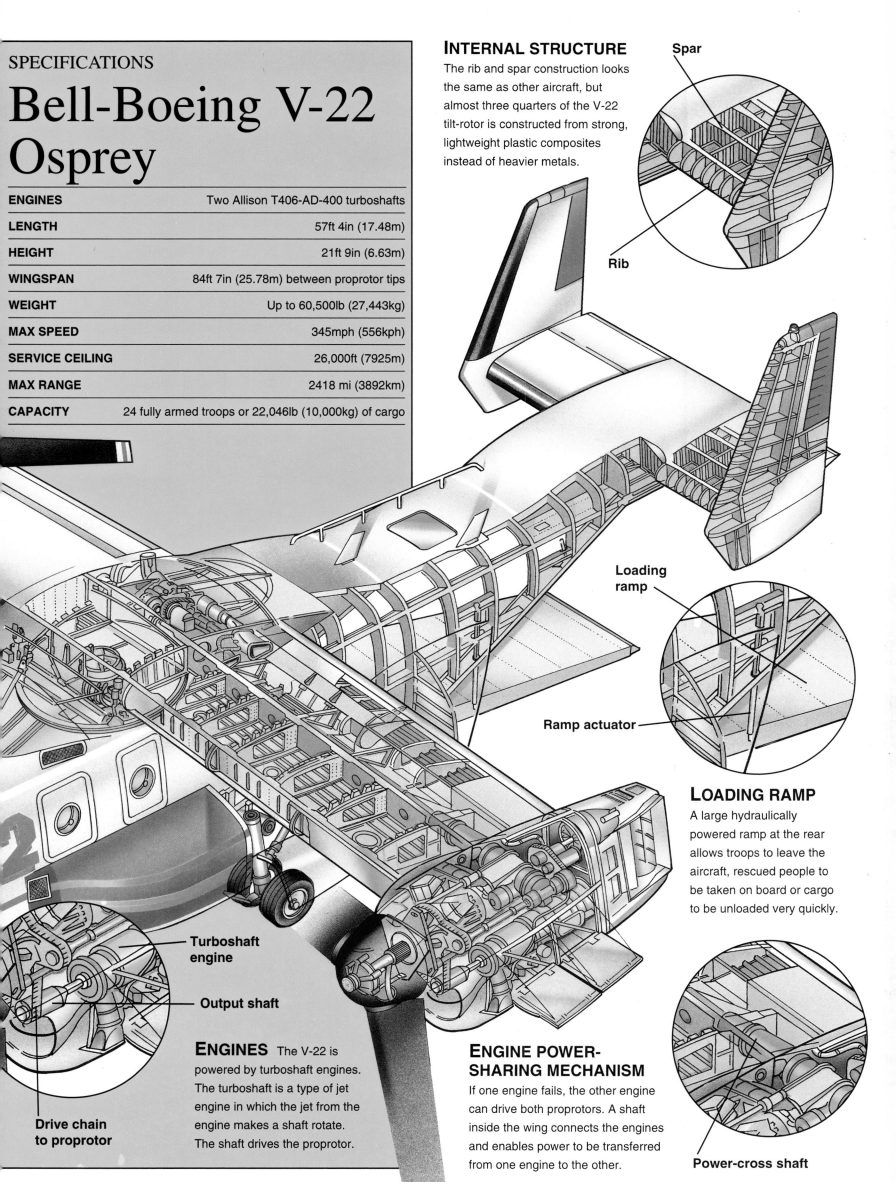

SPECIFICATIONS

Bell-Boeing V-22 Osprey

ENGINES	Two Allison T406-AD-400 turboshafts
LENGTH	57ft 4in (17.48m)
HEIGHT	21ft 9in (6.63m)
WINGSPAN	84ft 7in (25.78m) between proprotor tips
WEIGHT	Up to 60,500lb (27,443kg)
MAX SPEED	345mph (556kph)
SERVICE CEILING	26,000ft (7925m)
MAX RANGE	2418 mi (3892km)
CAPACITY	24 fully armed troops or 22,046lb (10,000kg) of cargo

INTERNAL STRUCTURE

The rib and spar construction looks the same as other aircraft, but almost three quarters of the V-22 tilt-rotor is constructed from strong, lightweight plastic composites instead of heavier metals.

Spar

Rib

Loading ramp

Ramp actuator

LOADING RAMP

A large hydraulically powered ramp at the rear allows troops to leave the aircraft, rescued people to be taken on board or cargo to be unloaded very quickly.

Turboshaft engine

Output shaft

Drive chain to proprotor

ENGINES
The V-22 is powered by turboshaft engines. The turboshaft is a type of jet engine in which the jet from the engine makes a shaft rotate. The shaft drives the proprotor.

ENGINE POWER-SHARING MECHANISM

If one engine fails, the other engine can drive both proprotors. A shaft inside the wing connects the engines and enables power to be transferred from one engine to the other.

Power-cross shaft

15

Helicopter

HELICOPTERS ARE USED for jobs that fixed-wing aircraft are unable to do. They can fly into the heart of a city and land on a tiny helipad; they can also operate from forest clearings because they can take off and land vertically. If necessary, they can hover in one spot or move forwards extremely slowly. Helicopters are used for tasks such as carrying passengers, inspecting power lines and oil pipelines, spraying crops and tracking people and vehicles. Most helicopters are powered by turboshaft engines, a type of jet engine in which the jet from the engine makes a rotor shaft rotate. Some small helicopters, however, have piston engines.

The Robinson R-44 is an example of a small piston-engined helicopter. Its engine is housed behind the passengers and fully enclosed to give the helicopter a smooth, streamlined shape. Sound-absorbing materials help lower engine noise levels in the passenger compartment. A large window in each of the four doors gives the pilot and passengers a clear view to the side and beneath them. The R-44's six-cylinder engine can speed it along at up to 149mph (240kph). Dual controls are fitted so that it can be flown from either of the front seats.

Blade root

Rotor attachment

ROTOR HEAD The rotor head links the engine to the rotor blades. To fly up or down, the pilot adjusts the collective pitch control lever. This pushes the swash plates, which are connected to the rotor blades via the rotor pitch levers. The pilot moves the cyclic pitch control lever to fly forward, backward or to the side. This twists the swash plates, which then tilt the rotor blades.

Rotor pitch lever

Swash plate

ROTOR PYLON
This holds the rotor blades clear of passengers that are boarding.

CONSOLE
Instruments showing the helicopter's height, speed, heading and position are housed in the console.

PILOT'S CONTROLS

The pilot flies the helicopter by means of four controls. Raising the collective pitch control lever makes the helicopter rise into the air. Twisting its handgrip, the throttle, makes the engine run faster or slower. Pushing the cyclic pitch control lever in a particular direction makes the helicopter fly in that direction. Pushing the pedals on the floor makes the helicopter turn.

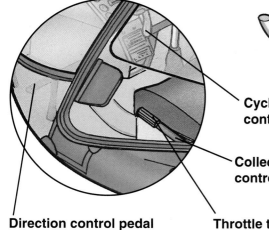

Cyclic pitch control lever

Collective pitch control lever

Direction control pedal

Throttle twist grip

LANDING SKID
This is mounted on energy-absorbing struts to withstand heavy impact.

Strengthening ring

TAIL BOOM The tail boom performs two functions. It holds the tail rotor at the correct distance from the main rotor and also houses the drive shaft which carries engine power to the tail rotor. It needs to be strong enough to support the weight of the drive shaft and withstand the turning forces it produces.

Drive shaft to tail rotor

SPECIFICATIONS
Robinson R-44

ENGINE	Textron Lycoming O-540 six-cylinder piston engine
LENGTH	38ft 5in (11.7m)
HEIGHT	10ft 9in (3.26m)
MAIN ROTOR DIAMETER	33ft 1in (10.1m)
WEIGHT	2398lb (1088kg)
MAX SPEED	149mph (240kph)
CRUISING ALTITUDE	Up to 13,944ft (4250m)
MAX RANGE	397mi (640km)
CAPACITY	Pilot plus three passengers

ROTOR BLADE
Each blade is 16ft 5in (5m) long and weighs 531lb (24kg).

RADIO AERIAL
The two radio aerials are angled backwards to streamline them and reduce drag.

Drive shaft

Gearbox

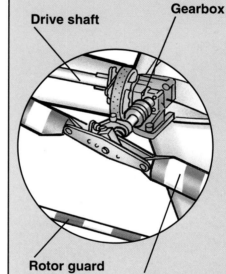

TAIL ROTOR
The tail rotor prevents the helicopter from spinning in the opposite direction to its main rotor by creating a balancing sideways push. It is powered by a drive shaft that runs along the tail boom from the engine. The R-44's tail rotor is 4ft 10in (1.47m) in diameter.

Rotor guard

Tail rotor blade

Cylinder

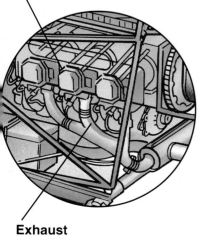

ENGINE The Robinson R-44 is powered by a 205 hp, six-cylinder piston engine. It works in the same way as a car engine. Air is sucked into each cylinder and compressed by a piston. Fuel is sprayed in and ignited. The hot gases that are produced push the pistons, which turn the drive shafts. These turn the rotors.

Exhaust

ROTOR GUARD
The guard stops the tail rotor from touching the ground during low level maneuvers.

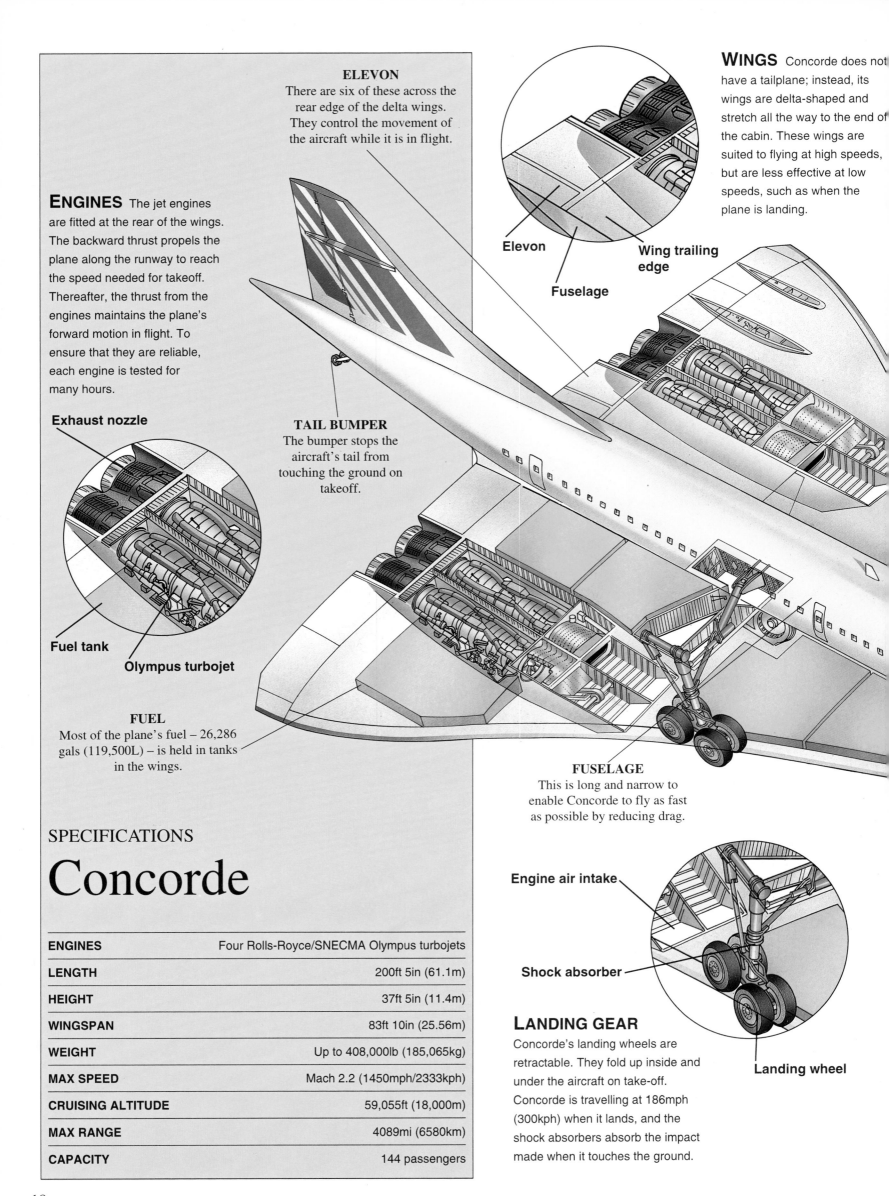

ELEVON
There are six of these across the rear edge of the delta wings. They control the movement of the aircraft while it is in flight.

WINGS Concorde does not have a tailplane; instead, its wings are delta-shaped and stretch all the way to the end of the cabin. These wings are suited to flying at high speeds, but are less effective at low speeds, such as when the plane is landing.

Elevon

Wing trailing edge

Fuselage

ENGINES The jet engines are fitted at the rear of the wings. The backward thrust propels the plane along the runway to reach the speed needed for takeoff. Thereafter, the thrust from the engines maintains the plane's forward motion in flight. To ensure that they are reliable, each engine is tested for many hours.

Exhaust nozzle

TAIL BUMPER
The bumper stops the aircraft's tail from touching the ground on takeoff.

Fuel tank

Olympus turbojet

FUEL
Most of the plane's fuel – 26,286 gals (119,500L) – is held in tanks in the wings.

FUSELAGE
This is long and narrow to enable Concorde to fly as fast as possible by reducing drag.

Engine air intake

Shock absorber

SPECIFICATIONS
Concorde

ENGINES	Four Rolls-Royce/SNECMA Olympus turbojets
LENGTH	200ft 5in (61.1m)
HEIGHT	37ft 5in (11.4m)
WINGSPAN	83ft 10in (25.56m)
WEIGHT	Up to 408,000lb (185,065kg)
MAX SPEED	Mach 2.2 (1450mph/2333kph)
CRUISING ALTITUDE	59,055ft (18,000m)
MAX RANGE	4089mi (6580km)
CAPACITY	144 passengers

LANDING GEAR
Concorde's landing wheels are retractable. They fold up inside and under the aircraft on take-off. Concorde is travelling at 186mph (300kph) when it lands, and the shock absorbers absorb the impact made when it touches the ground.

Landing wheel

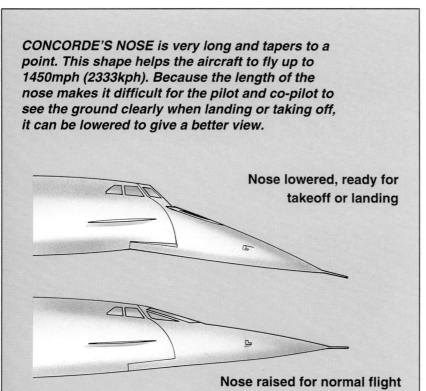

Nose lowered, ready for takeoff or landing

Nose raised for normal flight

Supersonic airliner

A SUPERSONIC AIRCRAFT flies faster than the speed of sound. The jet-powered airliners of the early 1950s flew as fast as 621mph (1000kph) – much faster than their propeller-driven predecessors. But by the late 1950s aircraft were designed which could fly faster than the speed of sound. The world's first supersonic airliner was Concorde, a joint production by the French and British aerospace industries. The slim, paper dart wing shape and four Olympus turbojets enable Concorde to fly high in the atmosphere at twice the speed of sound. Its top speed of 1450mph (2333kph) is even faster than many jet fighters. When flying west across the Atlantic, it crosses the sky faster than the sun, making it possible for travellers to arrive on the other side of the Atlantic earlier than the time they left! You can leave London at 11a.m. and arrive in New York at 9a.m. on the same day (using local times, of course). The journey only takes three hours, less than half the time taken by a long-range airliner such as the Boeing 747. Concorde flies at a height of 59,055ft (18,000m) – almost twice as high as a subsonic airliner. Although it first flew in 1969 and entered service in 1976, Concorde is still the only supersonic airliner in service.

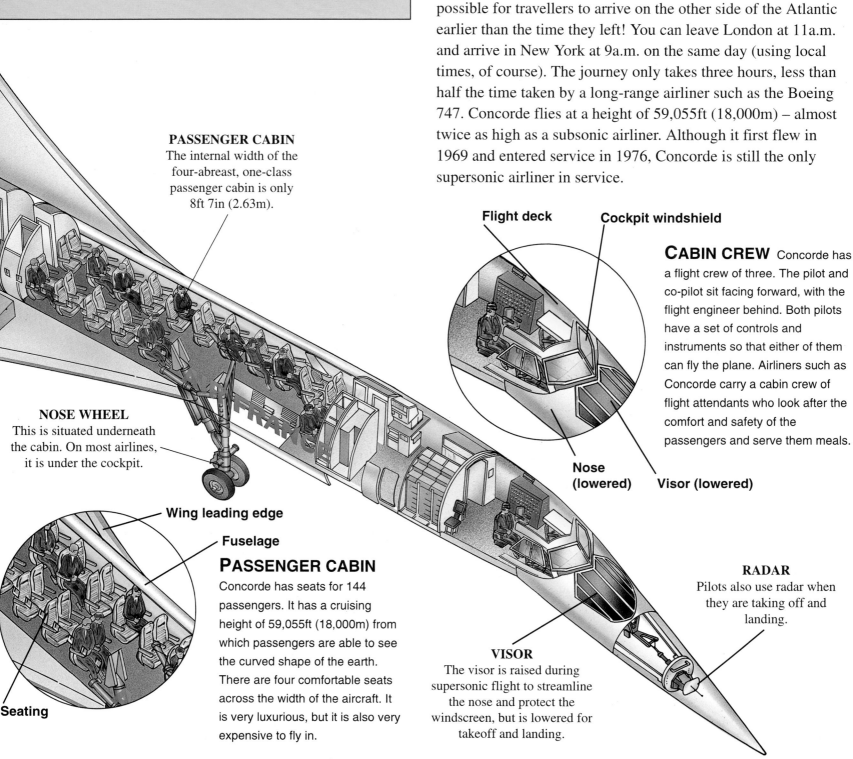

PASSENGER CABIN
The internal width of the four-abreast, one-class passenger cabin is only 8ft 7in (2.63m).

NOSE WHEEL
This is situated underneath the cabin. On most airlines, it is under the cockpit.

Wing leading edge

Fuselage

PASSENGER CABIN
Concorde has seats for 144 passengers. It has a cruising height of 59,055ft (18,000m) from which passengers are able to see the curved shape of the earth. There are four comfortable seats across the width of the aircraft. It is very luxurious, but it is also very expensive to fly in.

Seating

Flight deck

Cockpit windshield

CABIN CREW Concorde has a flight crew of three. The pilot and co-pilot sit facing forward, with the flight engineer behind. Both pilots have a set of controls and instruments so that either of them can fly the plane. Airliners such as Concorde carry a cabin crew of flight attendants who look after the comfort and safety of the passengers and serve them meals.

Nose (lowered)

Visor (lowered)

RADAR
Pilots also use radar when they are taking off and landing.

VISOR
The visor is raised during supersonic flight to streamline the nose and protect the windscreen, but is lowered for takeoff and landing.

Stealth fighter

STEALTH AIRCRAFT ARE military planes designed to avoid radar. They do this by absorbing and deflecting enemy radar signals so that the signals are not reflected back to their source, therefore revealing the location of the plane. Stealth aircraft achieve this in two ways: first, the plane is made from metal coated with a special material that absorbs some of the radar signals that strike it; second, the body and wings are shaped and angled to reflect the remaining radar signals away from their source.

The F-117A has flat, angled surfaces with sharp edges. It has a V-shaped tail and pyramid-shaped body with swept-back wings. All of its doors have serrated edges to prevent radar reflections. The position of the engines is important because the rapidly rotating fan blades could be picked up by radar, so they are set well back into the body of the plane with long inlet and exhaust ducts to deflect and absorb radar signals. Their position also protects the plane against attacks by heat-seeking missiles.

ENGINES The F-117A is powered by two General Electric F404-FD2 jet engines. The engines sit in the middle of the plane's body on either side of the two weapons bays. The engines are positioned deep inside the plane so that their heat and vibrations cannot be detected by missiles.

Weapons bay

Turbofan engine

Engine air intake fan

COCKPIT The F-117A is a one-seater aircraft with a pyramid-shaped cockpit situated in the plane's nose. There is very little space above the pilot's head, although there is plenty of room around his feet. The windshield is made from radar-absorbing glass.

WEAPONS BAY
The doors of the weapons bay are jagged, to help deflect radar.

Windshield

Pilot's harness

Engine throttle controls

AIR DATA SENSOR
Four small air data sensors feed information to the flight controls.

SURFACE
The black skin of the aircraft is a spray-on radar-absorbent material. This acts as a sort of cloak, concealing the aircraft by soaking up incoming radar waves.

THE NORTHROP B-2 Stealth Bomber avoids detection in the same way as the F-117A. Its shape and coating reduce its radar reflection to one hundredth that of a B-52 bomber (a large non-stealth aircraft). The engine intakes and exhaust outlets are mounted on top of the wings to shield them from detection by radar or infra-red sensors from below.

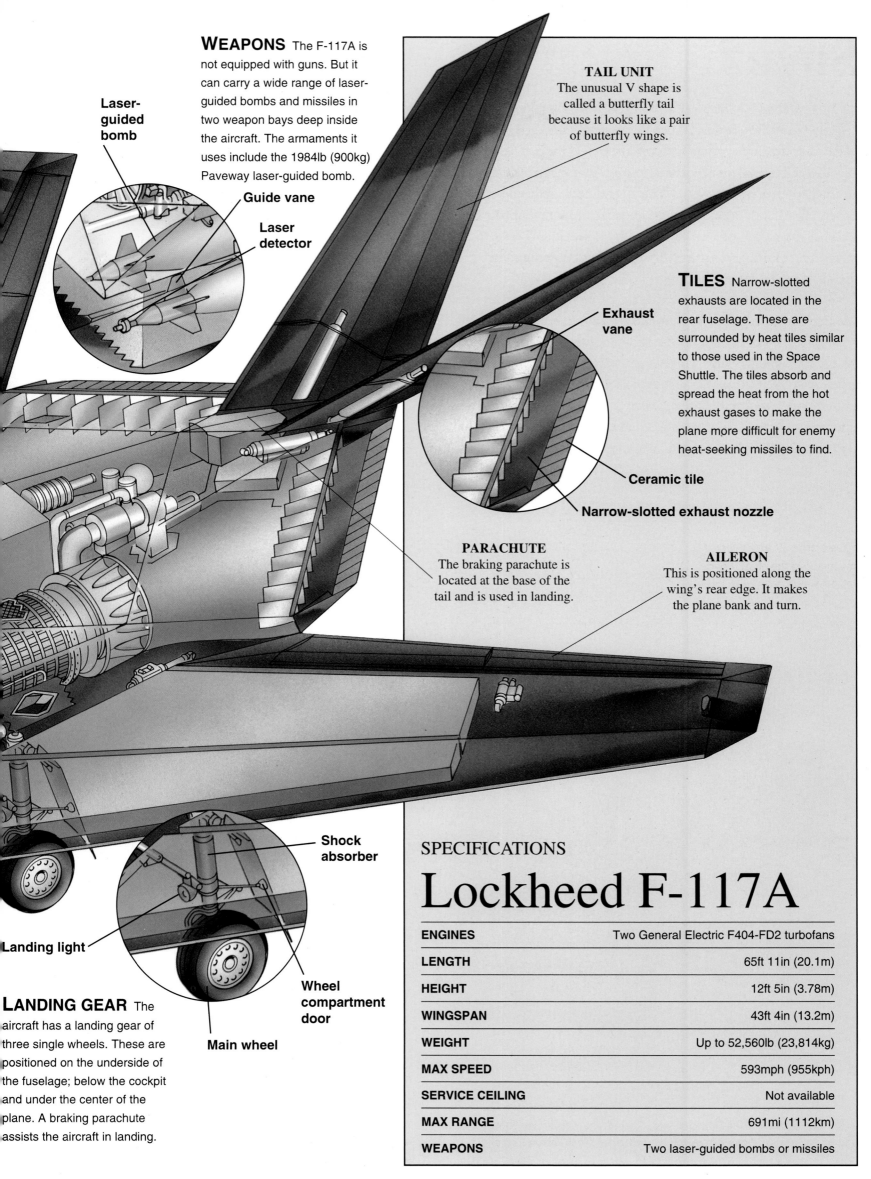

WEAPONS The F-117A is not equipped with guns. But it can carry a wide range of laser-guided bombs and missiles in two weapon bays deep inside the aircraft. The armaments it uses include the 1984lb (900kg) Paveway laser-guided bomb.

Laser-guided bomb

Guide vane

Laser detector

TAIL UNIT
The unusual V shape is called a butterfly tail because it looks like a pair of butterfly wings.

Exhaust vane

TILES Narrow-slotted exhausts are located in the rear fuselage. These are surrounded by heat tiles similar to those used in the Space Shuttle. The tiles absorb and spread the heat from the hot exhaust gases to make the plane more difficult for enemy heat-seeking missiles to find.

Ceramic tile

Narrow-slotted exhaust nozzle

PARACHUTE
The braking parachute is located at the base of the tail and is used in landing.

AILERON
This is positioned along the wing's rear edge. It makes the plane bank and turn.

Shock absorber

Landing light

LANDING GEAR The aircraft has a landing gear of three single wheels. These are positioned on the underside of the fuselage; below the cockpit and under the center of the plane. A braking parachute assists the aircraft in landing.

Wheel compartment door

Main wheel

SPECIFICATIONS

Lockheed F-117A

ENGINES	Two General Electric F404-FD2 turbofans
LENGTH	65ft 11in (20.1m)
HEIGHT	12ft 5in (3.78m)
WINGSPAN	43ft 4in (13.2m)
WEIGHT	Up to 52,560lb (23,814kg)
MAX SPEED	593mph (955kph)
SERVICE CEILING	Not available
MAX RANGE	691mi (1112km)
WEAPONS	Two laser-guided bombs or missiles

Soyuz

IN THE MID-1960s, the former Soviet Union developed a new type of spacecraft called Soyuz, meaning 'Union'. This was bigger than the earlier Soviet spacecraft, which were called Vostok and Voshkod. Soyuz could carry a crew of up to three cosmonauts into Earth's orbit and achieved several space "firsts", including the first docking of two manned spacecraft and the first exchange of crew members between two spacecraft in orbit. The basic Soyuz craft has been updated and changed to suit the needs of particular space missions.

There have been ten different versions of the Soyuz spacecraft, but their basic layout has remained the same. They all have three sections. The command, or re-entry, module is in the middle, and is the only part that returns to Earth. The egg-shaped orbital module is attached to it at one end. This contains life support equipment and provides extra space for the crew while they are carrying out their experiments. An access tunnel links the two sections. At the other end, the equipment module contains rocket motors and fuel; this is discarded when the command module returns to Earth. All but two versions have solar panels to produce electricity for their instruments.

On 17 July 1975, a Soyuz spacecraft docked with an American Apollo craft using a specially designed adaptor. Soyuz spacecraft are still used today to ferry cosmonauts to Mir.

BY THE TIME A SOYUZ spacecraft touches down, the recovery crew are already heading for the landing site. They help the cosmonauts out through the top.

ROCKET SECTION

The equipment module contains the spacecraft's rocket section. Two liquid fuel engines are used to move the craft to a higher or lower orbit and to slow it down so that it falls out of orbit and begins its descent to Earth. A separate, less powerful, rocket system is used to make fine adjustments to the spacecraft's position. The crew cannot enter this part of the spacecraft.

Rocket motor

Rocket propellant tank

EQUIPMENT MODULE

SOLAR PANELS

Electrical power is generated by two solar panels which fold out from the equipment module after launch. Each panel is 12ft (3.66m) long and covered by solar cells which convert sunlight into electricity.

Solar panel

External electrical connection

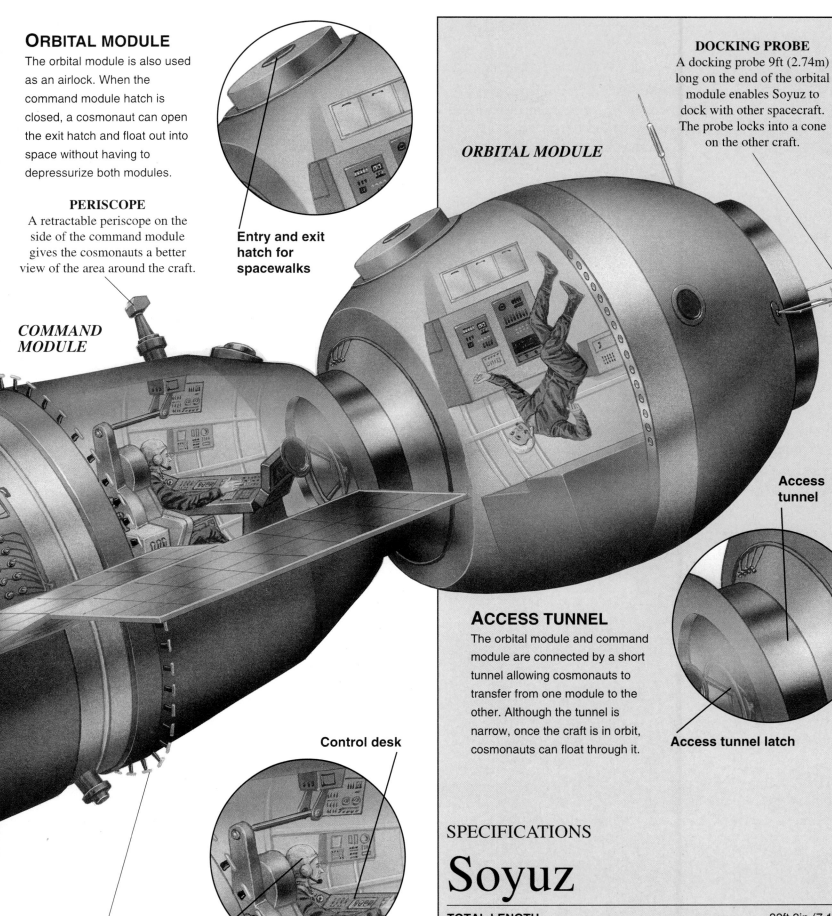

ORBITAL MODULE

The orbital module is also used as an airlock. When the command module hatch is closed, a cosmonaut can open the exit hatch and float out into space without having to depressurize both modules.

PERISCOPE

A retractable periscope on the side of the command module gives the cosmonauts a better view of the area around the craft.

COMMAND MODULE

Entry and exit hatch for spacewalks

DOCKING PROBE
A docking probe 9ft (2.74m) long on the end of the orbital module enables Soyuz to dock with other spacecraft. The probe locks into a cone on the other craft.

ORBITAL MODULE

Access tunnel

ACCESS TUNNEL

The orbital module and command module are connected by a short tunnel allowing cosmonauts to transfer from one module to the other. Although the tunnel is narrow, once the craft is in orbit, cosmonauts can float through it.

Access tunnel latch

Control desk

Cosmonaut

TELEMETRY ANTENNAE

A ring of radio aerials around the command module transmits information about the spacecraft to its ground controllers on Earth.

COMMAND MODULE

The command, or re-entry, module houses the spacecraft's control center. Its bell shape allows it to be flown in a controlled way through the atmosphere during re-entry. A heat shield on its blunt end protects the cosmonauts from the high temperatures produced by re-entry.

SPECIFICATIONS

Soyuz

TOTAL LENGTH		23ft 3in (7.1m)
TOTAL WEIGHT		Up to 15,432lb (7000kg)
TOTAL WORKSPACE		318cu. ft (9cu. m)
Command Module	DIAMETER	7ft 3in (2.2m)
	LENGTH	6ft 7in (2m)
	WEIGHT	6172lb (2800kg)
Orbital Module	DIAMETER	7ft 3in (2.2m)
	LENGTH	8ft 8in (2.65m)
	WEIGHT	2645lb (1200kg)

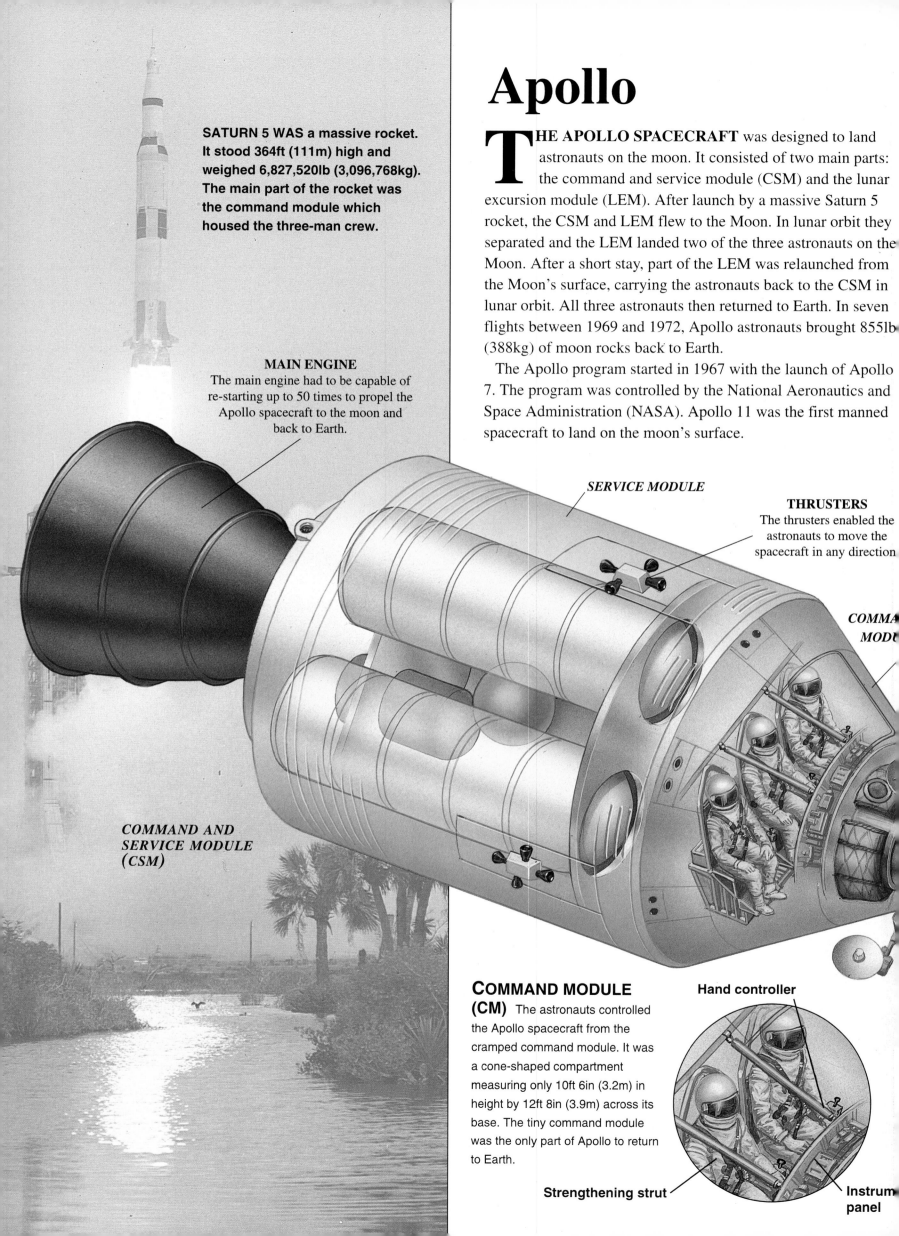

Apollo

THE APOLLO SPACECRAFT was designed to land astronauts on the moon. It consisted of two main parts: the command and service module (CSM) and the lunar excursion module (LEM). After launch by a massive Saturn 5 rocket, the CSM and LEM flew to the Moon. In lunar orbit they separated and the LEM landed two of the three astronauts on the Moon. After a short stay, part of the LEM was relaunched from the Moon's surface, carrying the astronauts back to the CSM in lunar orbit. All three astronauts then returned to Earth. In seven flights between 1969 and 1972, Apollo astronauts brought 855lb (388kg) of moon rocks back to Earth.

The Apollo program started in 1967 with the launch of Apollo 7. The program was controlled by the National Aeronautics and Space Administration (NASA). Apollo 11 was the first manned spacecraft to land on the moon's surface.

SATURN 5 WAS a massive rocket. It stood 364ft (111m) high and weighed 6,827,520lb (3,096,768kg). The main part of the rocket was the command module which housed the three-man crew.

MAIN ENGINE
The main engine had to be capable of re-starting up to 50 times to propel the Apollo spacecraft to the moon and back to Earth.

COMMAND AND SERVICE MODULE (CSM)

SERVICE MODULE

THRUSTERS
The thrusters enabled the astronauts to move the spacecraft in any direction.

COMMAND MODULE

COMMAND MODULE (CM) The astronauts controlled the Apollo spacecraft from the cramped command module. It was a cone-shaped compartment measuring only 10ft 6in (3.2m) in height by 12ft 8in (3.9m) across its base. The tiny command module was the only part of Apollo to return to Earth.

Hand controller

Strengthening strut

Instrument panel

Apollo

Service Module	DIAMETER	12ft 9in (3.9m)	
	LENGTH	24ft 7in (7.5m)	
	WEIGHT	52,636lb (23,876kg)	
Command Module	DIAMETER	12ft 9in (3.9m)	
	LENGTH	10ft 6in (3.2m)	
	WEIGHT	12,319lb (5588kg)	
	SPLASHDOWN WEIGHT	11,648lb (5283kg)	

Lunar Excursion Module		
	Descent Stage	*Ascent Stage*
DIAMETER	13ft 9in (4.2m)	13ft 9in (4.2m)
LENGTH	10ft 6in (3.2m)	12ft 5in (3.8m)
WEIGHT	22,045lb (10,000kg)	10,295lb (4670kg)

ASCENT STAGE

The ascent stage was launched from the descent stage platform. It carried the two astronauts from the Moon to rejoin the orbiting command module. Once the astronauts were safely aboard the command module, the ascent stage was set adrift.

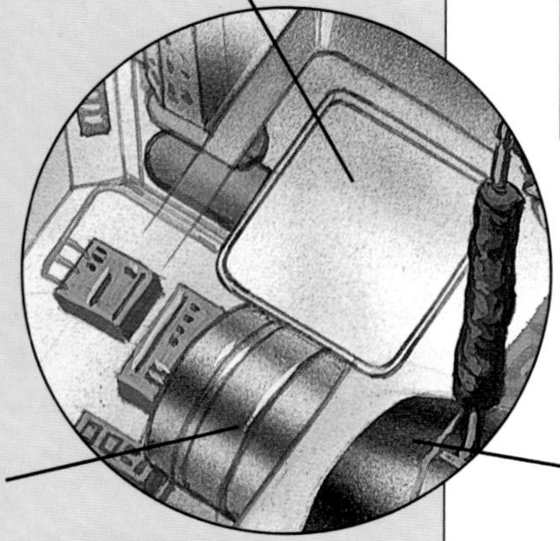

ASCENT STAGE

Exit hatch

Ascent engine

Ascent engine nozzle

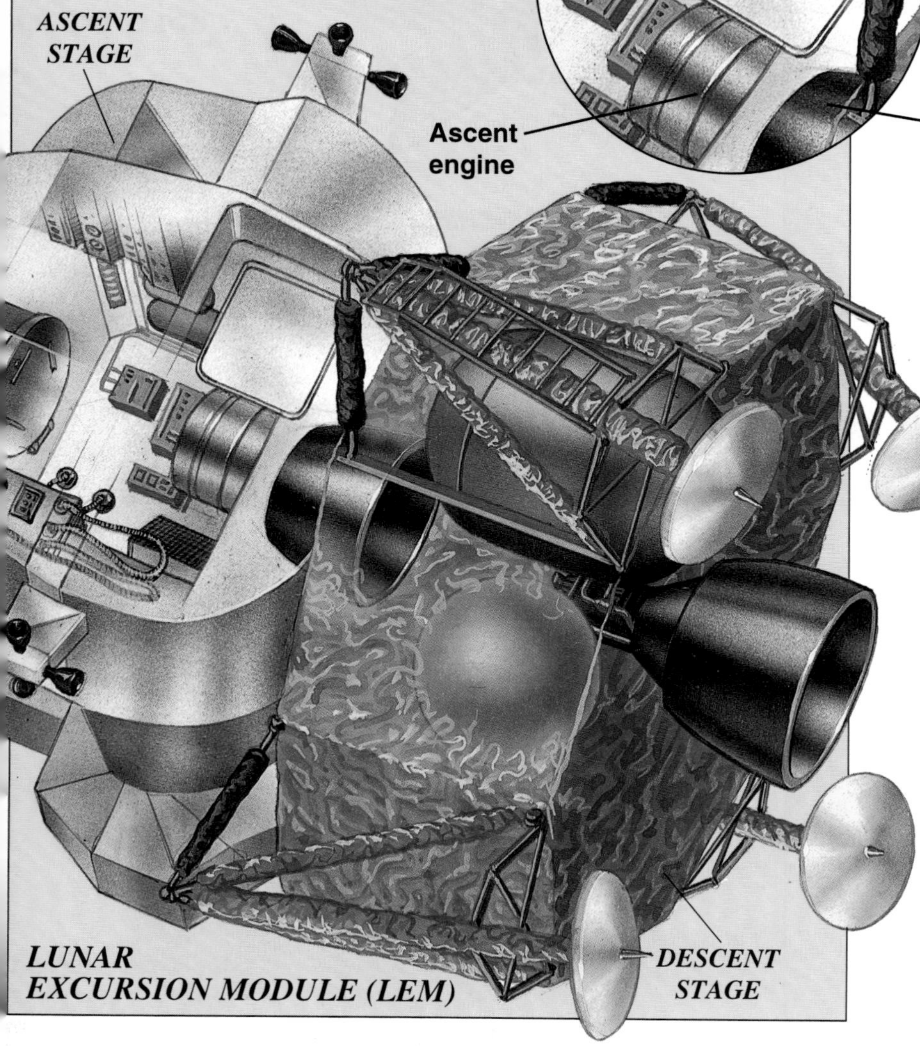

LUNAR EXCURSION MODULE (LEM)

DESCENT STAGE

NEIL ARMSTRONG and Edwin "Buzz" Aldrin were the first men on the moon. Aldrin is seen here walking on the moon's surface, next to the lunar module known as Eagle.

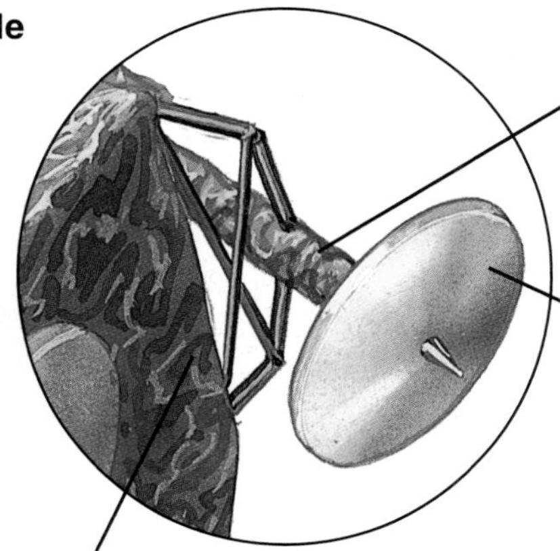

Landing leg

Footpad

Insulating gold foil

DESCENT STAGE

The descent stage's spider-like legs touched down on the moon and supported the LEM while the astronauts explored the surface and carried out experiments. It then provided the platform for the launch of the ascent stage, which took the astronauts back to the orbiting command module.

Space shuttle

THE SPACE SHUTTLE is the first-ever reusable spacecraft. Until 1981, when the space shuttle made its first flight, satellites, space probes and astronauts were launched by a rocket which was used only once. The space shuttle can be used over and over again. It consists of an orbiter craft, two solid rocket boosters and a huge external fuel tank that supplies the orbiter's engines. The orbiter itself is designed to be launched up to 100 times. It takes off like a rocket and glides back to Earth to land on a runway. There is now a fleet of four orbiters – *Columbia*, *Discovery*, *Atlantis* and *Endeavour*. *Columbia*, shown here, made the first space shuttle flight in April 1981. A fifth orbiter, *Challenger*, was destroyed in an accident just after it was launched in January 1986, killing its crew of seven.

Soon after the space shuttle is launched, its booster rockets run out of fuel and fall into the Atlantic Ocean, where they are collected by ships. They are then refilled with fuel and used again to launch another shuttle. The external fuel tank is the only part of the space shuttle that is not reused. When it is nearly empty, it falls back to Earth. It tumbles through the atmosphere and burns up.

The shuttle's large payload bay can carry satellites, equipment for experiments or even a manned space laboratory into orbit. Sometimes, astronauts on the shuttle collect faulty satellites that are in space to repair them.

PAYLOAD BAY

The orbiter's cargo hold is 60ft (18.3m) long. When its doors are opened, radiators inside them help to keep the orbiter cool by letting unwanted heat escape into space. There is no air in the payload bay when the orbiter is in space, so astronauts can only enter it through an airlock after putting on a spacesuit.

Payload bay door

Payload containe

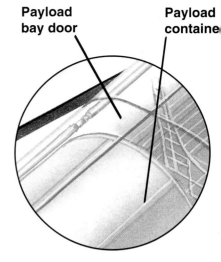

SOLID ROCKET BOOSTER

Two solid-fueled rockets, each standing 149ft 3in (45.5m) high, fire for the first two minutes of each flight.

RUDDER

The rudder steers the orbiter on its way down through the atmosphere toward its landing site.

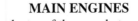

COLUMBIA *PREPARES TO LAUNCH its first satellite (SBS-3) in 1982. When the satellite is released, springs push it out into space. At a safe distance from the orbiter, its rocket engine fires to boost it into a higher orbit.*

MAIN ENGINES

A cluster of three rocket engines help to blast the orbiter into space. They fire for about the first 8½ minutes of each flight.

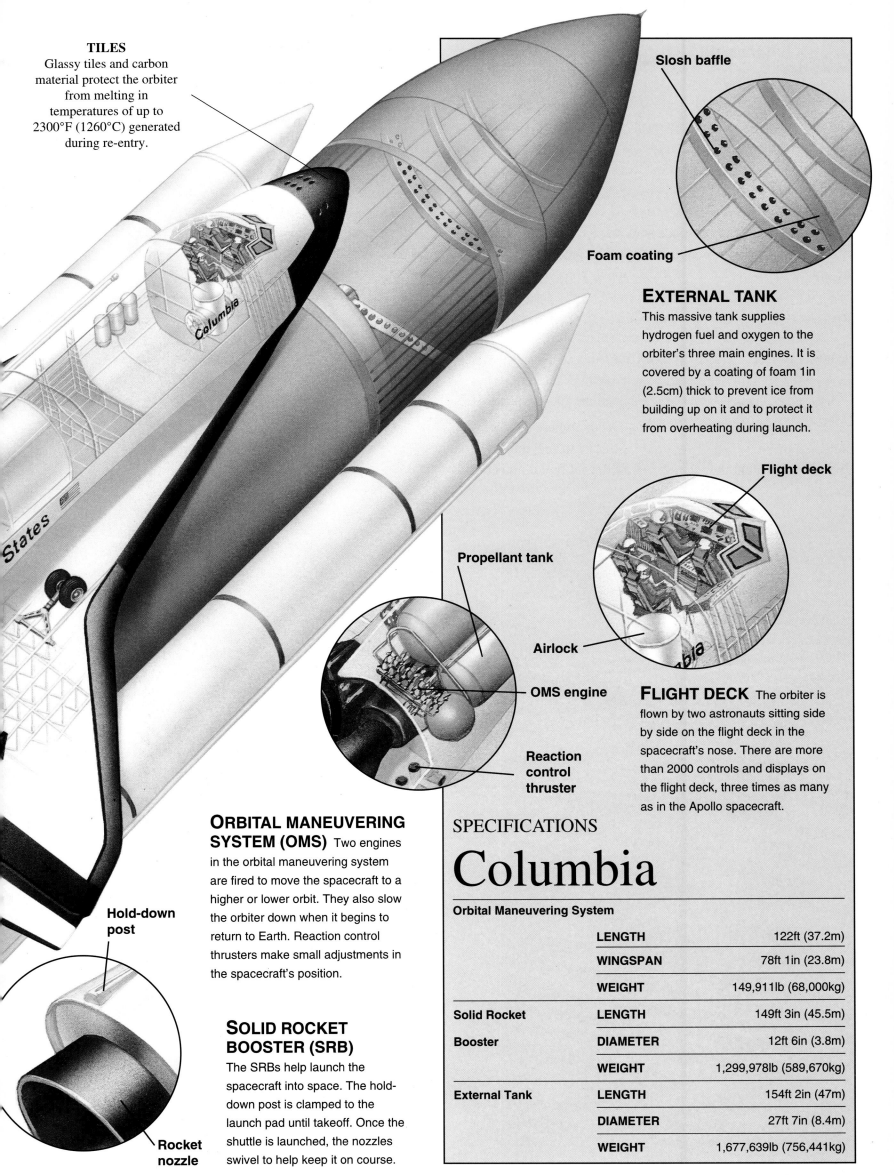

TILES
Glassy tiles and carbon material protect the orbiter from melting in temperatures of up to 2300°F (1260°C) generated during re-entry.

Slosh baffle

Foam coating

EXTERNAL TANK
This massive tank supplies hydrogen fuel and oxygen to the orbiter's three main engines. It is covered by a coating of foam 1in (2.5cm) thick to prevent ice from building up on it and to protect it from overheating during launch.

Flight deck

Propellant tank

Airlock

OMS engine

Reaction control thruster

FLIGHT DECK The orbiter is flown by two astronauts sitting side by side on the flight deck in the spacecraft's nose. There are more than 2000 controls and displays on the flight deck, three times as many as in the Apollo spacecraft.

Hold-down post

ORBITAL MANEUVERING SYSTEM (OMS)
Two engines in the orbital maneuvering system are fired to move the spacecraft to a higher or lower orbit. They also slow the orbiter down when it begins to return to Earth. Reaction control thrusters make small adjustments in the spacecraft's position.

SOLID ROCKET BOOSTER (SRB)
The SRBs help launch the spacecraft into space. The hold-down post is clamped to the launch pad until takeoff. Once the shuttle is launched, the nozzles swivel to help keep it on course.

Rocket nozzle

SPECIFICATIONS

Columbia

Orbital Maneuvering System		
	LENGTH	122ft (37.2m)
	WINGSPAN	78ft 1in (23.8m)
	WEIGHT	149,911lb (68,000kg)
Solid Rocket	LENGTH	149ft 3in (45.5m)
Booster	DIAMETER	12ft 6in (3.8m)
	WEIGHT	1,299,978lb (589,670kg)
External Tank	LENGTH	154ft 2in (47m)
	DIAMETER	27ft 7in (8.4m)
	WEIGHT	1,677,639lb (756,441kg)

Salyut

BETWEEN 1971 AND 1982, the former Soviet Union placed seven Salyut space stations in orbit around the earth. Salyut (which means 'Salute' in Russian) were used for both civilian research and as military space stations. Salyut 4, shown here, was a civilian space station. It continued research on space station systems and equipment that had been started on earlier Salyut space stations. Salyut 4 contained much more scientific equipment than any of its predecessors. It was occupied for a total of 93 days by two Soyuz crews – Soyuz 17 and 18. The Soyuz 18 crew lived in Salyut 4 for 63 days, which was a record at that time.

Large structures such as space stations can be kept in orbit around the earth for as long as the fuel supply for their engines lasts. After that, they gradually slow down due to the friction caused by collisions with particles from the outer fringes of the atmosphere, and start to re-enter the atmosphere. Salyut 4 fell back to Earth on February 3, 1977. It was positioned so that any parts which were not burned up during reentry fell harmlessly into the Pacific Ocean.

SOLAR PANELS

Electricity for the Salyut space station's life support system, its instruments and its experiments, was generated by up to four wing-like solar panels. Salyut 4 had three large steerable solar panels. Rotating joints meant that they could be turned to face the sun. When Salyut passed into the Earth's shadow, batteries supplied it with electricity.

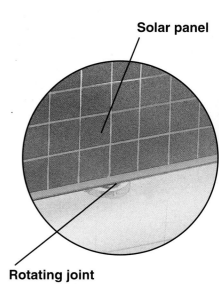

Solar panel

Rotating joint

COMMUNICATIONS

Aerials extending from the outside of the space station and its Soyuz ferry craft were used for radio communication and navigation.

Entry hatch

TRANSFER TUNNEL

An airlock compartment 9ft 10in (3m) long by 6ft 7in (2m) across allowed cosmonauts to enter and leave Salyut safely. Cosmonauts also transferred from visiting Soyuz ferry craft into Salyut through this tunnel-like compartment.

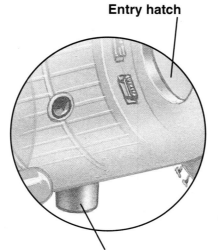

Navigation instruments

SOYUZ FERRY

Cosmonauts traveled to Salyut and returned to Earth again at the end of their mission in Soyuz spacecraft.

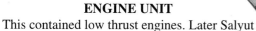

ENGINE UNIT

This contained low thrust engines. Later Salyut space stations could be maneuvered by docking unmanned Progress craft (modified Soyuz spacecraft) with them, and firing their engines. This saved Salyut's own fuel supplies.

WORKSHOP

Salyut had a large workshop and living quarters. This consisted of two cylinders, one 9ft 6in (2.9m) in diameter and the other 13ft 5in (4.1m) in diameter. The two cylinders were linked by a cone-shaped section, giving a total workshop length of 29ft (9.1m).

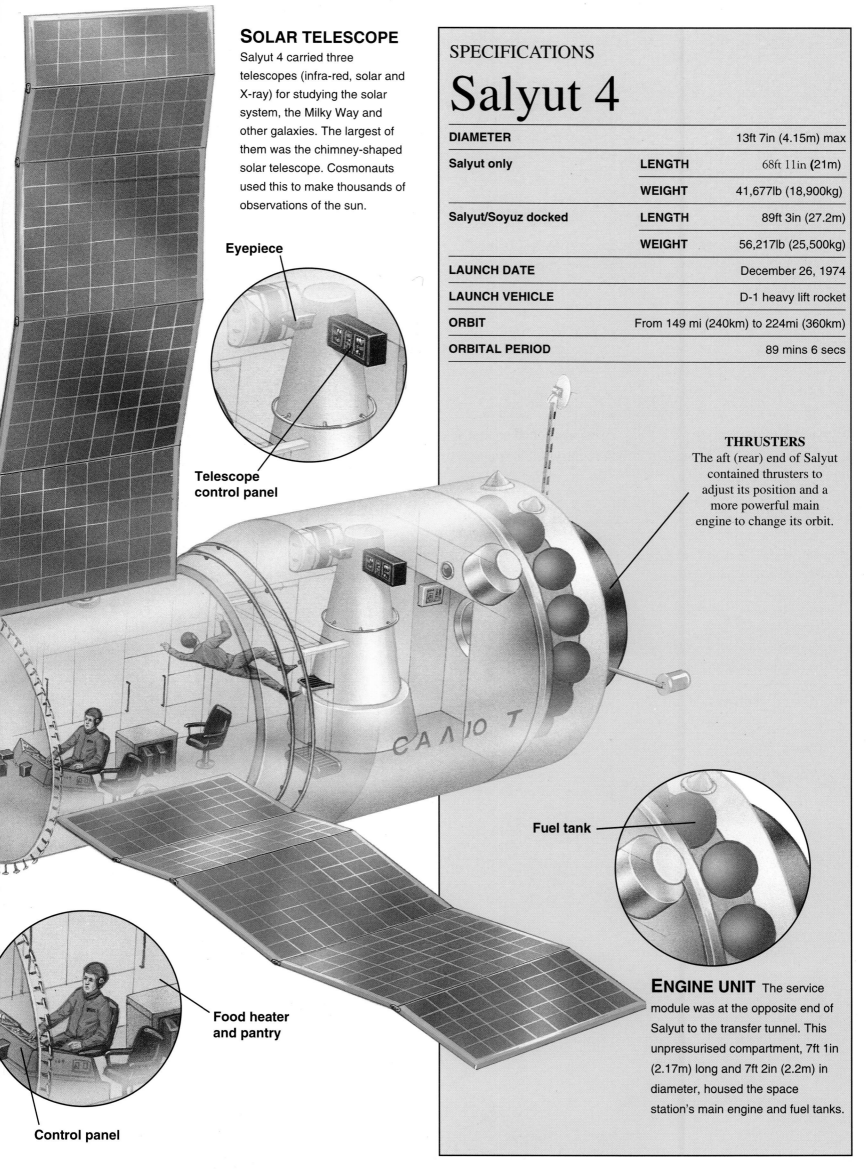

SOLAR TELESCOPE

Salyut 4 carried three telescopes (infra-red, solar and X-ray) for studying the solar system, the Milky Way and other galaxies. The largest of them was the chimney-shaped solar telescope. Cosmonauts used this to make thousands of observations of the sun.

Eyepiece

Telescope control panel

SPECIFICATIONS

Salyut 4

DIAMETER		13ft 7in (4.15m) max
Salyut only	LENGTH	68ft 11in (21m)
	WEIGHT	41,677lb (18,900kg)
Salyut/Soyuz docked	LENGTH	89ft 3in (27.2m)
	WEIGHT	56,217lb (25,500kg)
LAUNCH DATE		December 26, 1974
LAUNCH VEHICLE		D-1 heavy lift rocket
ORBIT		From 149 mi (240km) to 224mi (360km)
ORBITAL PERIOD		89 mins 6 secs

THRUSTERS

The aft (rear) end of Salyut contained thrusters to adjust its position and a more powerful main engine to change its orbit.

Fuel tank

Food heater and pantry

Control panel

ENGINE UNIT The service module was at the opposite end of Salyut to the transfer tunnel. This unpressurised compartment, 7ft 1in (2.17m) long and 7ft 2in (2.2m) in diameter, housed the space station's main engine and fuel tanks.

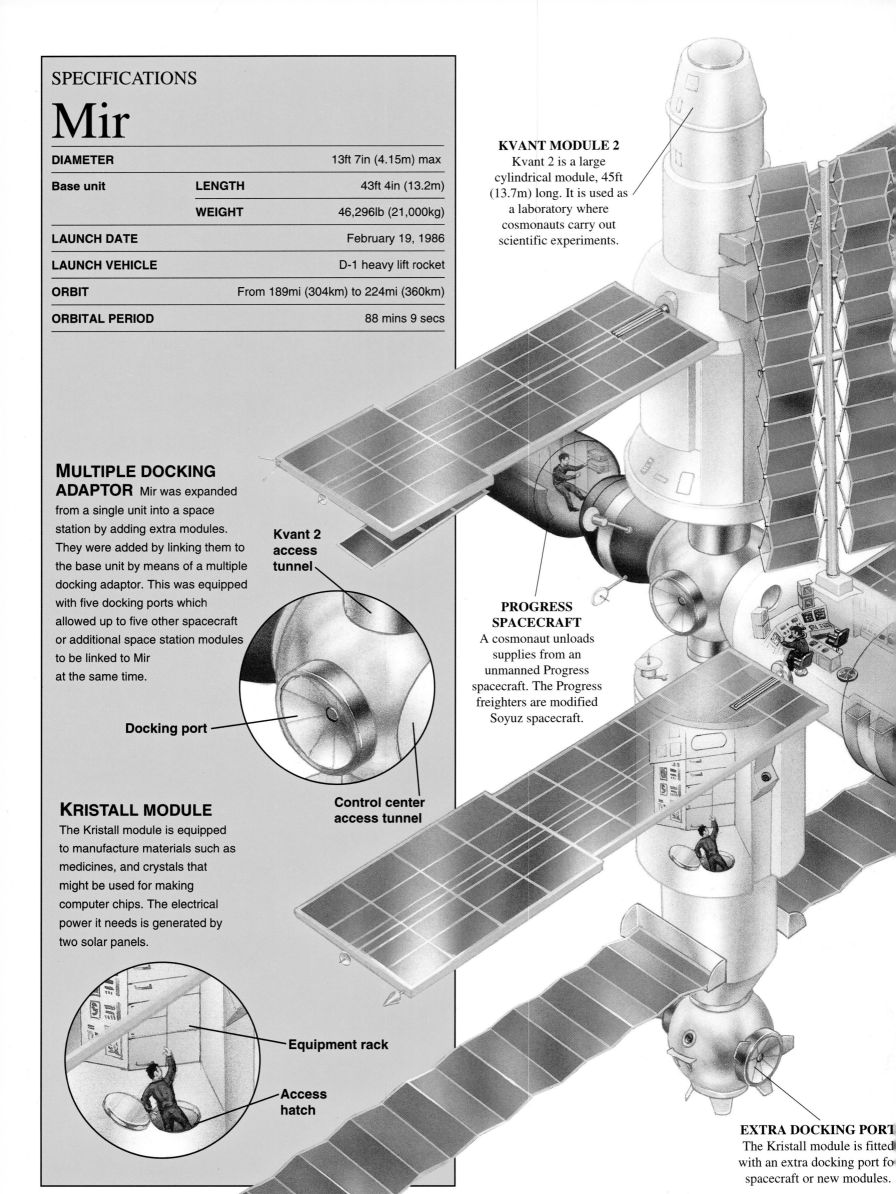

SPECIFICATIONS

Mir

DIAMETER		13ft 7in (4.15m) max
Base unit	**LENGTH**	43ft 4in (13.2m)
	WEIGHT	46,296lb (21,000kg)
LAUNCH DATE		February 19, 1986
LAUNCH VEHICLE		D-1 heavy lift rocket
ORBIT		From 189mi (304km) to 224mi (360km)
ORBITAL PERIOD		88 mins 9 secs

MULTIPLE DOCKING
ADAPTOR Mir was expanded from a single unit into a space station by adding extra modules. They were added by linking them to the base unit by means of a multiple docking adaptor. This was equipped with five docking ports which allowed up to five other spacecraft or additional space station modules to be linked to Mir at the same time.

Kvant 2 access tunnel

Docking port

Control center access tunnel

KRISTALL MODULE
The Kristall module is equipped to manufacture materials such as medicines, and crystals that might be used for making computer chips. The electrical power it needs is generated by two solar panels.

Equipment rack

Access hatch

KVANT MODULE 2
Kvant 2 is a large cylindrical module, 45ft (13.7m) long. It is used as a laboratory where cosmonauts carry out scientific experiments.

PROGRESS SPACECRAFT
A cosmonaut unloads supplies from an unmanned Progress spacecraft. The Progress freighters are modified Soyuz spacecraft.

EXTRA DOCKING PORT
The Kristall module is fitted with an extra docking port for spacecraft or new modules.

SOLAR PANELS

Mir's base unit and its modules use solar panels to generate the electricity that powers its systems and instruments. An extra solar panel was carried up to Mir inside Kvant 2 and installed in June, 1987 to generate even more electricity.

Mir

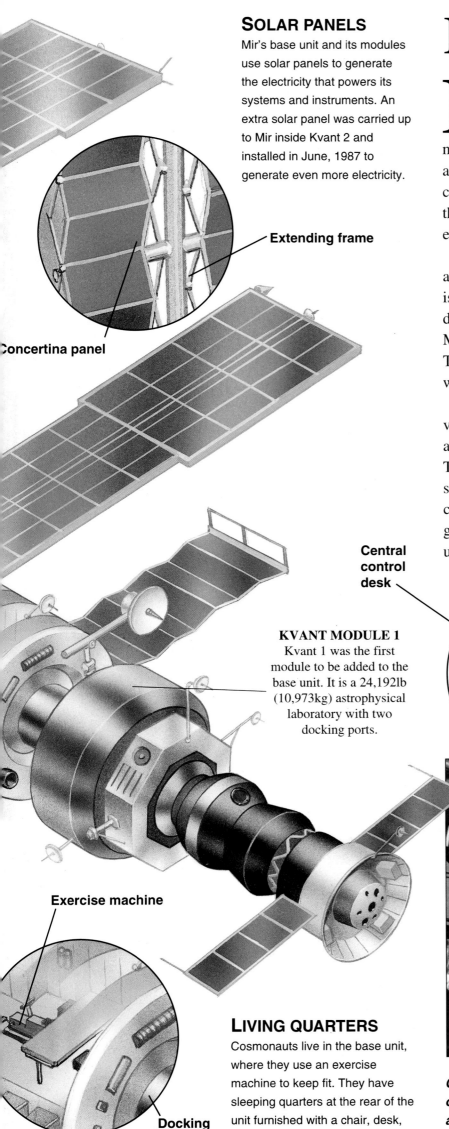

Extending frame

Concertina panel

Central control desk

KVANT MODULE 1
Kvant 1 was the first module to be added to the base unit. It is a 24,192lb (10,973kg) astrophysical laboratory with two docking ports.

IN 1986, THE FORMER Soviet Union launched a new type of space station which, unlike the earlier Salyuts, contained very little scientific research equipment. Mir, meaning 'peace' in Russian, was designed to be the base unit of a much larger space station. It provided living quarters for cosmonauts working on board the space station and also housed the control center. Other parts of the station housed the experimental equipment.

The base unit has six docking ports. A multiple docking adaptor at one end of the base unit provides five ports, and there is another port at the opposite end. These ports are used for docking add-on modules with the base unit. Spacecraft visiting Mir use the remaining available ports to dock with the craft. Two of the three add-on modules also have extra docking ports which can be used by visiting spacecraft.

Cosmonauts are ferried to and from Mir in an improved version of the Soyuz spacecraft, called Soyuz TM. Fuel, food and other supplies are delivered to Mir by Progress spacecraft. These are unmanned Soyuz vehicles stripped of their life support systems and heat shield so that they can carry more cargo. When they have been unloaded, they are filled with garbage and sent into the earth's atmosphere, where they burn up over the Pacific.

CONTROL CENTER

Mir is monitored and controlled by cosmonauts in the base unit. Its control desk contains all the displays, instruments and controls that are necessary for running the space station safely.

Exercise machine

LIVING QUARTERS

Cosmonauts live in the base unit, where they use an exercise machine to keep fit. They have sleeping quarters at the rear of the unit furnished with a chair, desk, sleeping bag and storage space.

Docking tunnel

COSMONAUT YURI ROMANENKO entered the Mir space station on February 7, 1987 and lived on board for 326 days, 11 hours and 38 minutes, setting a world record. Other cosmonauts have since set new records by living on Mir for more than a year.

Glossary

Aerofoil - A curved panel such as a wing designed to produce lift when it cuts through the air.

Air brake - A panel on an airborne aircraft wing which can be extended to catch the air flowing over the aircraft to slow it down.

Airlock - A compartment inside a spacecraft with one door to outer space and another door to the interior of the spacecraft. It allows space travellers to enter and leave a spacecraft without having to let all the air in the craft escape.

Astronaut - The name for a space traveller used in the United States and Europe. Astronaut means 'star traveller.'

Booster - A rocket used to provide extra thrust to help launch a spacecraft.

Console - A control panel.

Cosmonaut - The Russian name for a space traveller. Cosmonaut means 'a traveller in the universe.'

Docking - Linking two spacecraft.

EMU - Extra-vehicular Mobility Unit. A spacesuit with a life support system in a backpack used for spacewalks.

EVA - Extra-Vehicular Activity. Another name for a spacewalk.

Fairing - A streamlined covering.

Flap - A panel that extends from the rear, or trailing edge, of an aircraft's wing to make the wing bigger. This generates more lift so that the aircraft can land or take off more safely at low speeds.

Fowler flap - Basic flaps hinge down from a wing's trailing edge, but Fowler flaps move backward along tracks before they hinge down.

Heat shield - A panel fitted to a spacecraft to protect the craft from the extremely high temperatures produced when passing through the atmosphere at great speed.

Lift - The force created by the shape of a wing which sucks an aircraft upwards and enables it to fly.

Module - One complete part of a spacecraft or space station that can be separated from the rest.

Multiple docking adaptor - Part of a space station with two or more positions where spacecraft can dock.

Orbit - A route around a planet, star or other heavenly body.

Orbital maneuvering system - The pair of rockets used to change the space shuttle's orbit.

Orbital workshop - The part of the Skylab space station where astronauts work and carry out experiments.

Outrigger - A wing-tip wheel-strut used to balance an aircraft which has its main wheels positioned along its center-line.

Payload - Cargo carried by a spacecraft.

Radar - A system used to locate and track objects such as aircraft and spacecraft by bouncing radio waves off them and detecting the reflections.

Re-entry - A spacecraft's return to Earth through the atmosphere.

Retro-rocket - A rocket used to slow a spacecraft down and begin its return to Earth.

Satellite - An object in orbit around a planet. Moons are natural satellites. Spacecraft are artificial satellites.

Slat - A panel that extends from the front, or leading edge, of an aircraft's wing to make the wing bigger. This generates more lift so that the aircraft can land or take off more safely at low speeds.

Solar panel - A sheet of solar cells invented by the space industry for spacecraft to convert sunlight directly into electricity.

Sonic boom - The double-bang caused by a pressure wave created by an aircraft flying faster than sound.

Space probe - An unmanned spacecraft sent to explore outer space.

Splashdown - A method of landing a spacecraft in the sea used by American manned spacecraft.

Spoiler - A panel on an aircraft wing which can be extended on landing to 'spoil' the wing's ability to produce lift. This helps the aircraft to remain on the ground.

Stage - One part of a multi-stage rocket that has its own fuel tanks and rocket engines.

Subsonic - Slower than the speed of sound.

Supersonic - Faster than the speed of sound.

Thruster - A small gas-jet or rocket engine used to make small changes to a spacecraft's position.

Trajectory - The flight path followed by a spacecraft.

Turbofan - A type of jet engine.

Winglet - A small fin added to an aircraft's wing-tips to improve the wing's performance.